The Spirit of Creativity:

Embodying Your Soul's Passion

Karen A. Dahlman

THE SPIRIT OF CREATIVITY:
Embodying Your Soul's Passion

FIRST EDITION

A publication of CVC, Inc.
PO Box 1496
San Clemente, CA 92674
United States of America

Publish Date: November 2012

Artwork & Cover Design by: Karen A. Dahlman

In Gratitude of Spirit...

TABLE OF CONTENTS

FORWARD

The Spirit of Creativity: Embodying Your Soul's Passion is a timely book that addresses our growing needs to live the creative life. It reminds us that creativity is the energy of our life force and exists within every aspect of our lives. Creativity is not something you learn; it is something you are. This book helps you remember, reclaim, and embody your creative passion in tangible ways. Each of us has a unique way for expressing ourselves creatively, thus, you are encouraged to develop your own creative identity.

Ms. Dahlman teaches you that creativity is not a lofty ideal or something with which you must struggle. It is available to you; it is available to all! This message needs to be understood because creativity is the energy at the core of our being, the heartbeat of our soul, the backbone of our existence. With this understanding, you can engender the evolution of spiritual consciousness, personally and globally. You can learn to nurture your natural state of creativity.

The Spirit of Creativity invites you to tap into and unleash your own unique forms of creativity and evolve beyond the stereotypical belief that being creative is reserved only for the artistic elite. Through varying experiential exercises, including journal writing, art-making, visualization, meditation, and self-hypnosis you learn to incorporate and begin experiencing the flow of creative energy within your life. Ms.

Dahlman, through her background as an art psychotherapist and hypnotherapist, takes the mystery out of learning and applying these techniques on your own.

Within this book, you will learn suggestions on practical creativity that can expand the quality of your life. You will discover how to be creative without feeling intimidated, uncover the barriers that limit your experience of creativity, and reclaim and enhance your level of personal empowerment. In addition, keep reading to learn to incorporate creative expression within your daily routine, achieve greater clarity and insight by learning to use your intuition, and learn applicable suggestions to increase the experience of synchronicity within your life. We will explore how to begin living within the peace and flow of the creative Universe.

The Spirit of Creativity teaches you to address not only your heartfelt pursuits, but how to work with the painful emotions and situations that are inherent in life. The pain within your life should be explored and approached, not swept away or buried. Ignoring only promotes disease. Time-proven techniques are presented to help you delve deep into ways of channeling the unpleasant energy of our human condition for purposes of growth. Ms. Dahlman writes from a therapeutic, spiritual, and self-expansion perspective. This book will help you empower yourself to creatively express the magnificence of your soul. This is your time to welcome your creative legacy. This is your rightful inheritance.

INTRODUCTION

Many people—too many—believe they are not creative. To them, creativity seems beyond their reach. They believe it is something you must be born with and therefore, you either have it or you don't. Others believe they are somewhat creative, but only within limited areas. And then, of course, there are the few who actually know they are creative and readily and openly express their creativity within their life. We can venture a guess, though, that all of these people probably believe that creativity is only about being imaginative, artistic, or inventive. Well, isn't that so? Perhaps, but I will say this is only part of the truth.

There is more to creativity than meets the human eye. In fact, creativity surpasses the eye and dwells in the soul. The time has come to dispel our society's "creative myth," our current perceptions about creativity, and widen our understanding about the true nature of creativity. All of us can and must welcome our muse and live the creative life. When we are in touch with our creative nature, we bring ourself more fully in contact with the true essence of ourself.

The Spirit of Creativity is about nurturing your natural state of creativity. The creative ability is already within you, you just need to learn to open to it and allow its free unfolding. This book asks you to listen inward and learn to recognize your unique forms of creativity. The following pages take you, the reader, on an incredible journey inviting you into a place of inexhaustible and infinite vitality. This inviting place of creative spirit is full of vigor and life just waiting for your gentle awareness or your focused intent. This writing speaks about inspiration to be yourself, to channel your true expressions, to follow your own path, to live life to its fullest, and to open to your soul's purpose. I describe many core principles of creativity on the following pages. If you choose to put them into action in your life, prepare yourself for increased confidence and competence in all your pursuits!

When you are true to yourself,

these truths

cannot help but expand

into the other areas of your life.

This book is not about "how to techniques" to become a better artist or a more aesthetically expressive person than before. In fact, I don't believe we can make ourself more creative, just maybe more skilled. But it is about how to express yourself more openly and freely, uninhibited in your endeavors. I do, however, make suggestions and describe exercises you can put into practice as you learn to explore your creative calling. Therefore, this book is not about increasing one's artistic and inventive skills.

Throughout this book, you will be asked to reexamine and

expand your definition of creativity. You will be encouraged and challenged to bring forth into this world your own unique expression. The focus is to explore different concepts of creativity that can hinder it or enhance it. I highly recommend that you plan on keeping a journal that you can write and draw in as each chapter contains questions to ponder and experiential exercises to try. Other exercises, in the form of guided visualizations, are scripted in their entirety so you can create your own audio tapes. It's important not just to learn theory, but to have the opportunity for application.

The premise underlying the theme of this book is to remind all readers that everyone is creative. Everyone holds a piece of the puzzle to the Universal Masterpiece that is the ever-evolving process of Creation. Neglecting one's part is like losing part of the picture, a piece of the puzzle. The key is for all of us to find ways to own and express our inherent creative energy. I suggest many avenues and areas to tap into with each offering a different form of creative identification and expression. I do not offer answers—only possibilities. I offer insight and inspiration to help you reclaim your spiritual, creative essence, thus, find greater fulfillment in the greatest journey of all—life.

I present this book to you, inviting you upon an ever-expanding journey of creativity. I hope you explore these ideas but work with them in your own way as each person's path is as different as the next. I honor our uniqueness, yet admire our commonalities. It is within this interconnectedness that we can all learn to tap into creativity, but it is

through our uniqueness that we learn to express our own voice. We find

this voice at the essence of our soul where creativity lies.

Karen A. Dahlman
San Clemente, CA

Chapter 1 - THE CREATION SPIRIT

Long, long ago before the dawn of time as we know it, life existed as Spirit. Spirit was pure, potential energy. As Spirit imagined so it experienced. Spirit enjoyed working with its faculties of imagination. It knew that anything was and is possible. Great delight was found in creating.

To Spirit there was no such thing as limitation. It knew that the ability to express its creative essence was a God-given trait. Its pure, potential energy could express and experience anything. Everything was pure and everything was light, yet something was missing.

Spirit thought long and hard. It knew how to divide itself into many parts which provided interaction for itself. Loneliness was never an issue. Its purpose was to experience complete freedom and joy. That was what it did. Yet, it yearned for something not quite knowing what that something was.

This yearning created confusion. The confusion created chaos. Chaos created an opposite reaction to what Spirit was experiencing. Through Spirit's thought processes, it had created darkness. Spirit liked its creation as it could now experience the opposite of light. Soon after, Spirit began experimenting with duality, creating all kinds of opposites. This was fun. Spirit knew that the purpose of the opposites was to help itself have more balance within its realm. Spirit knew the truth. It yearned no more.

Spirit's awareness grew as it created. Spirit decided that it would permanently divide itself into many parts. It wanted to experience its new creations from many different perspectives. It knew that the more it divided itself, the greater its experiences. Spirit divided into countless reflections of itself in which each part mirrored the image of the whole. Interaction and expression was infinite. At the core of each image, Spirit placed an eternal, creative spark to remind the Spirit Parts of their inheritance.

As time moved on, the Spirit Parts experienced the pairs of opposites. However, the experience of each Part was different. The Parts began to diversify. As they began to diversify, they lost prior knowledge. They expanded further out and touched the edge of the galaxy. Many went on to create more galaxies and before long, the many Parts existed in expansive and infinite space. Knowledge was now diversified. Experience was now varied. Existence, as Spirit had originally known it, was now very different.

Spirit was content with its choice as it knew all would be constantly changing. It would be able to experience the process of evolution and growth. The many Spirit Parts continued developing. However, knowledge from whence they came and who they were had dwindled. Darkness had become frightening. Fear began to separate them. Many hid. They hid from their truths. Spirit knew this was the outcome of its choice. This was part of the plan.

Along the way there were those Spirit Parts who made their way back to truth by listening to the truth they heard within. This was their last remaining connection to Spirit. These brave Parts discovered it. Knowledge was never lost as previously assumed. Knowledge of the truth was just forgotten.

As their personal truths became known, the Spirit Parts knew that their existence was about the expression of their souls. Each Part was as important to the next Part as the next Part was important to another, and so on and so on. Each had its own creative essence needing to be shared with the others. Existence became a process of "re-membering," of putting back together the pieces of their true identity.

There were many Parts who cringed at any insight into the truth. They were still fearful. Others were just oblivious to their truths. That was all right as these were just other experiences to have and to grow from. Spirit knew that in time, all would awaken from their veil of illusion. Spirit knew that many would search everywhere for knowledge and forget to look within. That was just part of the plan. Spirit also knew that it would take not only a re-membering, but also a joining with others to fully understand their creative abilities. Eventually, all would awaken to their true inheritance. All would come to know their eternal, creative spark.

   And Spirit patiently waits….

Chapter 2 – CREATIVITY

MY CREATIVE UNDERSTANDING

Self-expression has always come naturally for me. When I was young, I bought into the belief that I was born creative. Back then, being creative meant that I must have had some type of skill and talent. Why else would classmates and others seek me out for ideas, drawings, poster creations, and various artistic endeavors? Others considered me creative because I could apply my artistic skill. I was learning in school that creativity was about artistry, talent and production.

While I was praised for my artistic ideas and supported in these creative pursuits, I was struggling with the term artist. I felt that my ability to be creative somehow encompassed more than being talented artistically. I just knew that there had to be more to being creative. This was ironic. In some ways, I felt like an impostor. In other ways, I felt like the struggling art student just trying to perfect the expression of my product. I became consumed by outcome as I forgot about the process. In school emphasis was placed upon aesthetics.

However, outside of school, in the privacy of my bedroom, I could spend hours upon hours playing with my stash of art supplies. I would play with textures, shapes, colors, and ideas. I was delighted by the process and usually surprised by the outcome. I liked my art the best when I did not plan. To me, this was the expression I loved, but it felt inferior to the graded art that lined the classroom walls. After all, classroom art was real art - at least that is what I thought!

All throughout my life, my repertoire for self-expression continued to develop and expand. I explored other forms of artistic self-expression, including writing, music, drama, and dance. I grew to understand that life was about experiencing myself in relationship to my environment in the many different ways I wanted to explore it. To me, this was being creative. Creativity was found in diversity and in the processes of learning and application. It was not found in the outcome. Creativity became an action word. It was not about skill and talent or pictures lining a wall. It was not just about the final product that others revered. It was about expressing myself in any way I enjoyed expressing myself. It was the experience that meant something, not the end result. This made sense.

Becoming an art therapist was a wonderful decision. It mirrored this understanding that I had learned earlier in the creative vessel of my bedroom. Creativity was about experiencing the process. Because we all are constantly in the process of transformation, I knew that creativity was available to all. We just need to experiment, take chances, and trust what our Inner Self knows it wants to express. Creativity could lead us to healing, insights, and understandings. We could access this in many ways.

My work as an art therapist has always centered around the

theme of helping others uncover their creative essence while learning to trust this process. I use the process of art-making as a metaphor serving people as a means for uncovering and rediscovering themselves. In some cases, people discover themselves for the first time through the art. My work has never been about diagnostics or interpretation. My work is not about being an artist. My work is not about talent or skill. It is about exploring one's life force. It is about tapping into one's personal well of creative energy: the essence of life

WHAT IS CREATIVITY?

Creativity is the spark of the soul. It is the glowing ember of our own, personal and unique expression. It is the passion that drives us and the energy that congregates within us, giving birth to our insights, dreams, and intuitions. Creativity is a force, a real and very powerful force of pure, potential energy relying upon our free will, the integrity of our choices, and the power of our beliefs to direct and focus its livelihood. The power of creativity lies within our hearts, not just in our hands. Production is not what creativity is about. Creativity entails the process and exists in the present moment. It is through our present thoughts and actions that we fuel the sparks of creativity. It is the journey that is of concern, not the destination.

We, as human beings, are creative beings constantly manifesting that which we know inside. We are all creative. We are creative beings because that is our true nature. That is the nature from which we were created. When we allow that creative nature of ourself to be expressed, explored inwardly and outwardly within our life, we are being creative; we are accessing creativity. When we feel the urge to express something, to move forward and expend energy, we are being creative. When we feel the bliss of being alive, we are being creative. Yet, the level and quality of creativity within our life depends upon how willing we are to tap into this energy, this pure force, and channel it with constructive integrity. Most likely, we are already open to expressing it within our life, at least to some degree.

Creativity is the energy that allows us to be ourself, that permits us to be unique, yet affords us the opportunity to be a part of a whole. Physical life, itself, is built upon millions of creatively organized systems, from the blood pumping through its network of vessels to the brain sending complex commands to muscles and organs. All of the varying systems and components of our bodies comprise our human form in its entirety, yet each whole formed by the sum of these parts is unique, differing from all other models of the human form. Each human being is related, but at the same time totally individual.

Creativity is the energy that flows through all life and through all expressions, connecting all together at the core. It is Spirit. However, creativity is also the energy that allows for the differences in an individual's experiences and expressions of it. This is the beauty of creativity, one energy, but as diverse as people in its outward forms.

Creativity is about life itself. It is about knowing and feeling that we are living life to its fullest, expressing ourself, voicing our song and dancing our dance

EVERYONE IS CREATIVE

Everyone is creative! We all have the ability to be full of passion in life. We all have the ability to express this passion outwardly. If we trace the word *creativity* to its Latin root, we find the root word *creare*, which translates as *to bring forth*. We all have the ability to bring forth our passion. Dictionary definitions in the present day tell us that being creative implies specific abilities that involve artistic or intellectual inventiveness. This definition focuses on the outcome or product of the creative endeavor. However, the original meaning of the word creativity does not focus on the product or outcome, but instead focuses on the process, the creative act itself, of bringing forth.

Creativity is a process. It is the process of bringing forth and expressing that which is inside of us. We cannot help but be creative when we are doing and being who we are, when we are activating and bringing forth our unique expressions of ourself within the world. These expressions are our gifts. We do a disservice to the world and in this case, to the Universe, when we do not share these gifts outwardly. We do ourself a disservice when we do not allow ourself to experience our expression(s) and others around us feel this great disservice too. When we express ourself by truly being who we are, which includes all of the aspects inside of ourself, we allow ourself to be within the flow of life. This flow is where creativity thrives. When we allow our creative juices to emerge fully, we are in the process of a creative act. We are in the presence of passion and awed by all of Creation.

Every single one of us has the ability to be creative. Our mere presence upon this planet, we call Earth, automatically bestows us the inherent rights to creativity. This physical world is a world built out of the actualization of creative expression. We live within a creative world thriving, when it is allowed full freedom, to express itself. Our world continually creates and recreates itself. Our world provides us the opportunity to do the same. What has happened, some where along the way, is that our culture has deemed only those (as the dictionary ascribes) who are inventive or perceived to be talented with a skill as being creative. Given this definition, only the artists are the ones who are creative. People are encouraged to be creative, but believe this misconception of the creative myth, that in order to be considered creative, we have to have a product or outcome to show, a way to measure our creative worth. This is not the case. Somehow, all of this has become misconstrued along the way. Creativity has become something you only do rather than someone you automatically are. This is far from the truth! Inside all of us is the potential creative energy readily waiting to be accessed and released. We are actually creative by our very existence, here in the flesh. Who we are is an expression of

24

ourself. When we are true to our soul's calling (our divine and inherent plan), we are being creative. We are bringing forth ourself into the world.

Creativity is about living fully aware, intensely in contact with the richness of ourself and open to the world of experiences. Being creative is about making a journey back to ourself and discovering the process involved and the awareness gained in doing so. When we realize that our inherent rights as a human being is being creative, is about bringing forth our unique Self, then this awareness opens us up to limitless possibilities. By expanding into the field of infinite possibilities, we begin to understand that we are not limited by what society deems as being creative, but that we are truly unlimited in the manner and ways in which we can express ourself. These include, but are not limited to being talented or inventive. Our understanding of what creativity is expands. We comprehend that we are creative by merely expressing our heart's desire. We learn to exist within the flow. We learn to express ourself in uninhibited and freeing ways. This liberating progression of understanding stems from expanding our perception of ourself as a creative individual, from allowing ourself free and full expression, and by listening to our heart's desire and following our soul's calling.

In my practice as an art therapist, I have met many, many people along the way who have professed to being uncreative. I would inevitably tell them that art therapy is not about being creative in the sense of painting an aesthetically pleasing piece of artwork, but it is about expressing oneself, which is the link to personal creativity. Like clockwork, this would always be followed up by the comment, "Well, I can't draw; I'm not creative." It was as if they thought that drawing was the only way to be creative. Now, our culture would tell us that we can be creative in writing, music, poetry, acting, dance, business, gardening, cooking, and teaching, to name a few, but it does not tell us that we can be creative by merely expressing what it is that is inside of us. Many of my clients, like many people I know, tend to believe that in order for them to feel creative they would have to be able to create some type of acceptable, tangible product displayed in front of them. They want something cool-looking and pleasing to show as their work, understandable, considering what we have all been taught to believe about creativity.

Throughout my practice as an art therapist, it is apparent that everyone has <u>their</u> <u>own</u> way to express oneself using the art media. There is never a right nor a wrong way of genuinely expressing oneself. When people are given this statement as the groundwork to a session, they more openly and more readily express themselves. Everyone has their own unique form and manner of self-expression and when people work in groups it is easy for all to begin encountering this. At first, there are always individuals wanting to hide their artwork in embarrassment and not wanting to share. As they stick with the process long enough, maybe after a few sessions or sometimes even after one session, they begin to experience the others' acceptance of what they are creating and expressing, both visually and verbally. Group members develop an honest desire to learn about the process each goes through as they are creating their artwork and as they are learning to genuinely express themselves. This always progresses into wanting to hear what another is experiencing, feeling, saying, and expressing. This accepting and nonjudgmental atmosphere allows many of these people to increase self-acceptance and learn to honor their own expressions with pride. My art therapy work is just one avenue for helping people tap into the awareness that there is energy inside of them that wants and needs to be brought forth.

Granted, in therapy, there is a lot of piled up garbage, baggage, leftovers, and debris that must be sorted through before the treasure, our true expression, can emerge. Yet, many times, even when the treasure is found and uncovered, we are frightened of its power. We are afraid of owning our own voice and standing our own ground no matter how promising and enticing this may sound. The notion of allowing ourself to express the full glory of who we truly are, can seem very overwhelming, thus intimidating. This is because true expressions bring power with it. Power within many of our lives has been experienced through misuse and abuse. We may have misused it or others have misused it around us. Many of us have been abused by it. This power and feelings of empowerment within becomes a seemingly scary thing. We have learned to fear power. Thus, we cut ourself off from our true creative expressions and our own empowerment.

Not too long ago, I was speaking with a handy-man who I hired to work in my house and fix a few items for me. He noticed all of my artwork adorning our walls. He was asking me about it and made the comment that he wished he too could be creative and how nice that would be if he was. I was dumbfounded by his comment because I really believed that what he was doing in my house required the capacity of creative thinking. He needed to access the situation, determine the materials and tools required to do the job, and finally, implement his ideas. This seems like a creative act as defined by our dictionary. I mentioned this to him and suggested that by being a handy-man and having the ability to figure out how something broken can be fixed requires intuitive and creative juices. Now, he appeared dumbfounded. His mouth opened, his eyes widened and he said, I've never thought about it in that way before! He left my home possibly believing that he was more creative than he had originally assumed and possibly owning his creative ability for the moment, and hopefully longer.

This is an example of what has happened within the human culture. People do not believe they are creative unless they can display a product deemed by others as aesthetically pleasing. What is being emphasized here is that creativity is not about a product or an outcome, but it is about the process of being open to the vast unlimited sources of images, ideas, thoughts, and emotions that are within us. When we are open to these concepts we allow this part of ourself to emerge. We do not stop the flow. We allow our Self to be brought forth. However, we tend to block this process. Judgments, concerns with perfection, and focus on outcomes stop us dead in our tracks and limit our creative process.

Our emotions are powerful components of this creative process. Our emotions can be broken down into *e-motions*. This means *energy in motion*. Motion is process. It is the act of doing. It is the act of being. Putting in motion or giving expression to this energy can free the spirit and promote powerful awareness and insight. By paying attention and being open to our emotions, we are setting our spirit free. When we experience intense emotions, we can learn to feel them, but not hold onto them nor fear them. Emotions are energy in motion and need to be released. They need to move. It is when we hold fast to them we experience the most pain. The process of allowing them to flow through us is most freeing and teaches us to understand the flow of energy.

Expressing who we are, expressing ourself, can be enhanced through literal energy in motion. For example, walking, driving, sailing, or even floating on water, among many other leisure activities, can help induce relaxed states of awareness. Relaxed states are altered states that help promote the creative flow. Many artists are familiar with this relaxed, trance-like state of mind when they create. This is when the painting paints itself, the poem writes itself, and the garden plants itself. This state is generally coupled with a loss in awareness of time. This is when time seems to stand still and we transcend the temporal. This is when we know we are in synch with the creative flow.

Life is a journey. Life is a process. There is no end result. Creative energy invites us to be in the process and to focus on the moment. It asks us to allow ourself to be who we came here to be, right here and right now, in the present. It is time to create. It is time for creativity to express.

Chapter 3 - GROUNDING CREATIVITY

The core of our being is a sacred space. It is the place within us where our connection with all of life is not only recognized, but is honored. This is the place where the essence of ourself, our creative Self, resides. It is through our connection to All-That-Is that we can experience the power of creative energy. When we understand how even our slightest thoughts influence and interconnect us with the functioning of our life, we take our creative responsibility more seriously. Therefore, it becomes important to prepare for the actualization of this creative energy within our physical world by understanding the inner workings of this potent energy.

To operate freely within this interconnection with All-That-Is, we must ground ourself first. We must establish firm roots into the soil of our intentions and convictions. We must be clear with ourself about what it is we desire and what it is we wish to express. Becoming clear with ourself will not be attainable until we feel centered and strong within ourself. Grounding helps us do this. Attaining this clear focus with clarity requires an inner exploration and an honest dialogue with oneself. This process takes time as we are continually growing, changing, and evolving.

WHY I NEED TO GROUND

It is important to establish a solid position, a "groundedness," within ourself in order to withstand the volatile nature of our world today. This means being able to feel a sense of inner stability all the while events, industries, and institutions are continuously shifting and changing all around us. This inner stability provides us with our sanity. It keeps us flexible and fluid, ready to exist within the world, but not controlled by the collective influence of the world nor at the mercy of these changes.

Being flexible and fluid, yet at the same time establishing a solid ground may seem contradictory. And in one sense, it is. Yet, when we discover the creative potential that lies within, we tap into a whole new meaning for strength. This threshold of inner strength is not made up of muscle and mass, but instead is comprised of a solid and strong relationship between the outer face we present and the inner truths we know. Exploring these inner truths cannot help but lead us to the building blocks, the basis, the groundwork of who we are. This takes us back to the core of ourself where our creative essence resides. This creative essence is of a sound nature, meaning that it is dependable and reliable, but only as so far as we open to it and allow its emergence. This is how the face we present, the hat we wear, the persona we exude becomes flexible and fluid. We learn not to try to control the changing events and circumstances around ourself. With patience and practice we develop a trust within ourself knowing we can provide and take care of ourself regardless of the change and uncertainty that abounds. We learn to believe in our inner strengths. This inner connection becomes solid, yet flexible and fluid.

We were never taught in basic science class that something can be solid (a particle) and fluid (a wave) at the same time. Quantum theory in modern physics teaches us that we are all comprised of subatomic units of matter vibrating at varying rates of speed giving our body the illusion of solidity when, in fact, our body is a massive, fluid pattern of particles. These particles have a dual aspect appearing solid or fluid, dependent upon how we view them. According to Fritjof Capra, professor of physics and author of The Tao of Physics, "Quantum theory has shown that particles are not isolated grains of matter, but are probability patterns, interconnections in an inseparable cosmic web." He further says, "Quantum theory thus reveals a basic oneness of the [U]niverse." It is important to understand that both states of being do, in fact, occur simultaneously, are interconnected, and create the patterns constituting the Universe.

We learn that having a "solid ground" does not mean being stubborn and that being "flexible and fluid" does not mean being spineless. It does mean, however, to begin establishing our roots of trust within our own inner strength and to begin bending with the winds of change. Did you know that the trees most likely to survive a turbulent wind storm are the ones that can bend? We can all learn a lot from this type of flexible strength.

HOW DO I GROUND?

When we explore ways to "ground" ourself, you might find it helpful to work with a visual image. The image for grounding oneself is ROOTS. Imagine yourself establishing firm and sturdy roots into the earth's soil, penetrating her layers of crust, when you are exploring the concepts in this chapter. Each chapter builds upon each other so it is important to lay the groundwork (no pun intended!) here.

Roots are important for the growth and development of vegetation. The system of roots secure the plant in place, pull nutrients from the soil, and provide water. Without roots, vegetation would not exist. The roots can be viewed as the plant's life support. It's life depends upon it's roots.

Now, imagine that your roots are also your life support; the basic foundation required to provide you with optimal functionality. As your roots reach down into the ground, feel your connection to the soil of your convictions. These convictions, these beliefs, are what grounds you in your life. These are the factors determining the structure and quality of your life. What we believe influences how we view life and life's unfolding story. So, we begin to ground ourself by exploring our current root structure, our beliefs.

Following is a visualization exercise intended to help you work with this principle of grounding yourself. Here, you will be using it as a way to explore your current belief (root) structure. This exercise serves as an example for how you can relax, feel connected, and grounded. In the future, you can curtail this visualization to meet your own needs. It can be used at any time you are feeling disconnected, unfocused, or flighty. You may even find that it can be used during the work day to provide a quick energy booster. Remember, you provide the nutrients to your soil.

Directions -

Read the visualization first, obtaining an idea of what it's about, then put the book down, close your eyes, and simulate <u>your own</u> version of this exercise. Most importantly, there is no one way or right way to do this. The idea is for you to use the suggestions, but develop your own wording, images, and understanding. After all, it is your own path that you are on.

<u>The Root Visualization</u>
(For grounding)

Allow yourself to get comfortable. Gently close your eyes. Take a deep breath. On the inhale gather up all worries. On the exhale release all the related tension, stress, and strain. At your own pace take several more breaths. When ready, imagine an energy source at the base of your spine. Feel the warmth of this energy radiating. Notice its color if you see one. This continual energy runs down your legs, out the soles of your feet, and into the earth. The energy takes on the shape

and structure of roots when it enters the earth. Feel your connection to

the ground through this expanding structure of roots, spreading out and

down, deeper and deeper, further down it goes. Now, notice how your

root structure exists. (Pause.)• Do you have many roots branching off

or maybe you have one large root extending from each foot? Do your

roots have space to grow? Do your roots grow near the surface much

like the roots of a cactus? Or do your roots grow deep and very large

like the roots of a redwood tree? Just notice and be aware of your roots.

You are connected to Mother Earth. You are grounded in the soil you

have provided for yourself. Maybe it's time to water the ground, maybe

it's time to fertilize. You add the necessary nutrients to the soil that

your root system needs at this time. Trust what it is your roots need to

help your body function optimally. Nurture your growth and

development. Take your time. (Pause.) Now that you are aware of

your roots and the space in which you are grounded, be open to

exploring the soil of your convictions. What are your beliefs about life?

What are your beliefs about yourself? About your work? Your family?

About prosperity? As you explore these beliefs and any others, ask

yourself if they serve you or hinder you. Be honest with yourself. Be

---

•   Notice the text for the visualization exercise is written with the pauses in place. This is for your benefit in case you want to create an audio tape of the exercise, reading it verbatim. All of the visualization exercises throughout the book include the pauses.

open. Take your time. (Pause.) Just tuck these thoughts away for now and focus on your breath. In and out, in and out. Bring your awareness back to your roots. Move your awareness up and up, out of the earth, following the stream of energy up your legs back to the base of your spine. Bring your focus back to the room where you are. When you are ready open your eyes. Stretch and remember what you experienced. Welcome back.

After any visualization, it is a good idea to write down or sketch your experience. Keep a journal dedicated to your visualizations and meditations. This practice helps reinforce the inner exploration you are doing. It sends a signal to your creative Self that you are taking your self-exploration seriously.

EXPLORING BELIEFS

Our beliefs, our convictions, influence how we view life, others, and ourself. Beliefs establish parameters and set boundaries for our perceptions and interactions. They determine how and whether or not we will approach something or abstain. Beliefs safely contain our life. We, as human beings, have the mental abilities to create beliefs. We also have the capability to adopt and amend our beliefs.

A belief is based upon one's faith and trust, whether it is in an establishment, in an idea, in a concept, or in an institution. A belief is merely energy that is congregated around a certain principle. The energy is, in a sense, focused and contained within a space creating a structure which we would then call a belief. A belief is the foundation upon which our environment is built. The foundation lays the grounding structure upon which we will build our mental home. A structure is a principle that tends to guide our life by means of influencing our attitudes, our thoughts, our perceptions, our behaviors, and our actions. A belief structure says a lot about an individual, from where the individual came and to where the individual is going. It says a lot about what is housed within an individual. Our personal environment and the atmosphere in which we live are built from the basis of our beliefs.

When we have a conviction about something, we believe strongly in it. As Franz Kafka, an Austrian novelist and short-story writer, said, "A belief is like a guillotine, just as heavy just as light." This statement sums up exactly how a belief can and will ultimately limit us regardless of how the belief may serve us. We tend to limit ourself because we think it will make us safer. If we can have everything in our life organized, neatly and orderly, compartmentalized, segmented, explained, understood, reasoned, interpreted, and analyzed, we think we will be safe. We want all of our ducks in a row. When we do this we are ascribing parameters to our world. We are actually building impenetrable walls without doors or windows. These walls limit and contain the expression of our creative soul. We are closing ourself down, shutting ourself off, walling out, and limiting our experience as a co-creator with the Universe flow. In essence, we are limiting our creative ability. Our beliefs are worthy of our examination, especially if these beliefs are cutting us off from experiencing life, others, and the flow of our own creative energy. No one wants to be labeled, thus limited, as a failure, a dumb person, or as a procrastinator, for example. We need to be careful how we perceive ourself and what we believe about ourself. As the Old Testament states, "As a man thinketh in his heart, so he is." A look at our self-beliefs is a must.

Let us explore how our own beliefs and the beliefs we hold about others or about life in general can affect us. If we believe that others are out there to get us, to short- change us, are of a dog-eat-dog world, then that is what we are going to find. What we believe influences our perceptions. For example, if you believe you are a "failure" then your perceptions about your interactions within life are tainted by the label failure. You might as well have written failure across your forehead because, in fact, that is what you have set yourself up to experience. Any other negating beliefs and for that matter, supporting beliefs, about ourself becomes our own truths. These are going to be the perceptions we carry with us as we move through life. When we are tainted by these types of perceptions, the way we carry ourself and interact with others is influenced. If we maintain the belief that money is scarce, for example, we may come to interact with life fostering this fear. We may become overly competitive and aggressively hostile toward others as we live for money or we may live in fear always scrounging and experiencing a lack of money. What we believe is what we will experience. An excellent book describing this concept in more detail is <u>You'll See It When You Believe It</u>, by Wayne Dyer, a psychologist and best-selling author. It's a concept worth studying.

How is it that different individuals can approach the same situation, yet have entirely different responses or outcomes from the situation? This happens because all of us hold different beliefs. We all have different ways to perceive a situation. I'm sure you have heard the old proverbial story of the three blind men exploring an elephant for the first time and describing what they find. One is feeling the trunk and exclaiming, "Wow, this elephant is really long and skinny, like a garden hose." Another is touching the tail and saying, "Yeah, it's really long and thin, and it's wispy at the end. It's like a painter's brush." Another man is feeling the elephant's body and saying, "Oh, this animal is huge and round like a giant barrel." Each one of these men has a different experience of what an elephant is because all of them have encountered a different perspective of the elephant. They encountered the same elephant, but just different aspects of it. What they know about the elephant is colored by their experience and their own perception of their experience. However, they are each only perceiving a part of the whole. We do this. We tend to base our beliefs upon our limited perspectives.

At some time, we have all entertained beliefs about another that we tend to hold onto as truths about this person. We may have met somebody who was "copping an attitude" (appearing to be rude and curt) and we labeled that person as a rude person not meriting of our company or our respect. If we believe that what we perceived, in this case, was a rude person, we will tend to interact with that person as the label deems fit. We don't like rude people, so we are determined to stay away and decrease interaction with this individual. We may even spread the word about this person's rudeness, furthering the label. Yet, there is another side to this picture. The supposedly rude person may have been having a bad day and the expressed rudeness was nothing personal, but unknowingly displaced frustration. There are most likely other people who know this so-called "rude" person as a very nice, amicable person and would never consider this individual as rude. We are tainted by our beliefs so we tend to interact with others accordingly.

If we can maintain a belief that we are spiritual beings, first and foremost, then we begin to expand the boundaries we have assumed for ourself. We are not only human beings evolving in life, but we are souls transcending our physicality. We have the capability within ourself to be who we secretly know we are. With this realization we may then become more forgiving, understanding, and compassionate to others, to life, and most importantly, to ourself. If we can be more forgiving, understanding, and compassionate to ourself, this will obviously extend into other areas within our life, especially in the lives of those with whom we interact. When we believe that we are infinite spiritual beings, this allows us more easily to examine our current beliefs in perspective. We can see how our beliefs may serve a purpose within the physical realm (such as making sense and bringing order to our world), but we can also discern how beliefs can limit our soul and spirit as to who we truly are at the core of our being.

During the "grounding" exercise you explored what some of your current beliefs are about yourself and about various areas within your life. You began to look at whether or not these beliefs serve you or hinder you. Now, let's explore what you want to believe about yourself, about your life, and about others. What kind of perceptions would you like to maintain? What are your convictions? These are important questions to ask yourself so you can begin to explore the areas in which you are limiting and/or containing the full expression of yourself, your being. One way to begin answering these questions is to answer the main question:

Who am I?

This is a question that has been asked many times worldwide by many different people from all eras and walks of life. So, it's time to ask yourself the same question: Who am I? Write your answer to this and the following questions in your journal. Pay attention to the type of words you use when describing who you are.

Do you describe yourself by your work, profession, and/or title?

Do you explain who you are by your relationship to others, e.g., parent, sister, spouse, boss, or friend?

Do you describe yourself by feelings such as caring, loving, honest, enthusiastic, or mellow?

Is who you are only described by these prescribed roles and conditions?

Who are you really? Is the way you portray yourself the way you truly are at your core?

Explore who you are by describing the many facets of yourself.

We already know that each of us is an infinite, spiritual being with magnificent beauty inside, wanting to be expressed within the world of form. Try describing who you are, now, by exploring this inner energy and empowerment.

If you could express the full essence of your being, how would you describe this essence?

How would you like your relationship with others to be?

How would you like your interactions with life to be?

What are the characteristics and qualities that you haven't fully allowed to be a   part of your existence?

These are questions to refer to when you explore yourself. But remember, the labels, the words, the thoughts, and the perceptions we have about ourself influence the quality of our life and the expression of our creative energy. How we perceive our environment, our life, and our world, becomes the channel influencing the flow of our creativity.

We may be damming it up or constricting the flow. How we harness or free this energy is up to each individual. We just need to examine our beliefs and choose carefully when we think or talk about who we are, who others are, and what life is about. In the end, what we expect and what we perceive is what we will get. What you believe is what you will find in life. It sets your limits and expands your horizons.

HOW DO I MOVE BEYOND LIMITING BELIEFS?

We move beyond our limits, our inhibitors, and our boundaries when we open ourself to the world of limitless possibilities, to believing anything can happen and that anything is possible. We tend to be limited only by our beliefs and by our perceptions. In other words, we are truly unlimited beings if and when we become aware of the infinite and limitless possibilities that exist within us. We can do this once we explore our beliefs about ourself and about our capabilities.

The dream realm shows us how anything can happen with a myriad of probabilities. When we dream, we have the ability to do anything, be anywhere, and be anybody. We solve our problems, gain insight, work through situations, release repressed energy, work out our frustrations, and perform various other activities while in the dream state. This is because the dream world is a realm of infinite possibilities. What you conjure up, you experience. It is possible for us, while in the waking state, to tap into this unlimited, infinite realm as well. This realm is only closed to us by our own mind. It is as limited as we make ourself limited. It is closed to us by our thoughts, by our beliefs, and by our perceptions. All of these processes originate from within the mind. How we use our mind is the limiting factor. We are physically limited by what we don't use, especially if the capability exists. We are limited by the level of consciousness we care to employ. The mind is not limited to the physical organ known as the brain. We do know that we use only a very small portion of our brain, however, the mind is not synonymous with the brain. The mind is of the brain and of the body, yet transcends the experience of the brain and body. The mind is an expression of the soul in the physical world. We must learn to engage this aspect of our soul. We can learn to live our dreams.

Throughout life we learn limits. We become very good at setting limits, developing parameters, establishing boundaries, setting restrictions, guidelines, regulations, and rules. We even begin to sanction the limitations we have created for ourself. But as you will find, there are always people out there who seem to experience so-called "extraordinary" events. Wonders that occur outside the parameters of our organized and rationalized life, such as winning the lottery, living out our dreams, communicating telepathically, or surviving a near death experience, are hard to believe. We attribute these "tours de force" to being miracles, pure luck, mere coincidences, or just being at the right place at the right time. Generally, we don't give the individual credit. However, if we began giving the individual credit for effecting these spectacular accomplishments, the individual would probably begin to believe that he/she could achieve these things again. When there is the persevering, boundless belief behind the thought or the intention, there is the result following shortly thereafter. With credit being given due, this individual will easily begin to believe that he/she can accomplish all kinds of things. When one individual can do it, others will soon believe they can too. Well, why not? Moving beyond limits becomes a contagious thing! Instead of this feat being considered extraordinary, it becomes the norm. This is not to make light of incredible accomplishments and miracles. This is only to say that these occurrences need to be and can be brought into the light where others can share in the experience of them more readily and freely.

We do this all of the time within the world of technology and science. Just take a look at the computer industry. The personal computer that sits on your desk or fits into your briefcase is more powerful than the computers that were in use forty to fifty years ago. These computers of yesteryear, each, originally occupied two floors of an office building. We really didn't know if an enormous decrease in size was possible many years ago, nonetheless, the technological advancement was never limited. This limitless thinking makes it possible for everyone, today, to own a personal home computer. Who would have dreamed 100 years ago that medicine and science would be implementing organ transplants on humans with kidneys, livers, hearts, you name it? How about space travel? Man has always dreamed about traveling to distant planets. It was in 1960 when President Kennedy declared his challenge to the American people that a man would walk on the moon before the end of that decade. In 1969, the culmination of hard work and focused efforts on the behalf of many witnessed Neil Armstrong's famous first words while he set foot on the moon, "One small step for man and one giant leap for mankind." Well, somebody dreamt it and these are realities of today. We don't appear to be limiting ourself in these areas of growth and development, so, why do we set limits for the growth and development of the mind of a human? Why can't the human also progress in a similar fashion? It's noted by research that we use approximately 5% of our physical organ, the brain. There is obviously more that this organ can do. Just imagine what heights we could possible reach if our brain and mind were fully used. If this expansion into infinite possibilities is imaginable for machines, apparatus, and techniques, why wouldn't it be thinkable for the human being?

In order to move beyond our limits, we need to look at what it is that limits us. Many different things in our life can limit us. Investigate where it is that you are placing limitations upon yourself. Do you hold limiting thoughts? How about limiting beliefs? Do you feel limited in your abilities even though the capability is present or do you limit yourself from even trying? Do you limit your own evolution and growth?

These are just a few ways we might limit ourself. We can become aware of how we are limiting ourself when we pay attention to our self-statements. These are statements we make about ourself, generally to ourself within our head, but we also make these statements outwardly in conversations with others. For instance, have you ever approached a new activity or event with the pre-judgment of failure in mind? You might have made the statement, "Gosh, I could never do that' or 'you won't get me out there' or 'this is stupid' or 'you've got to be crazy if you do that." These are examples of statements we make to ourself or to others that already limit our functionality within this activity before we even start. These statements can keep us from engaging and enjoying ourself in the activity or situation at hand. They can keep us from excelling at something or finding out that it is or truly isn't our cup of tea. We will never know until we engage and we will never know if we sabotage our efforts by destructive self-statements before we even try.

Paying attention to our self-statements is very important. Many times we don't even know that we are saying such things about ourself to ourself or to others. Have you ever attempted a diet only to find yourself struggling with the whole concept? Have you tried paying attention to your self-statements? Possibly, you're making the diet even more of a struggle by counteracting your attempts with self-sabotaging talk. Do you catch yourself saying things, such as, "I'll never lose the weight, I'll never get rid of this stomach pooch and these big thighs, It's hopeless, and I have fat genes?" Well, of course you won't lose the weight if you believe you can't or you aren't going to. It becomes a losing battle no matter how hard you try because your beliefs about yourself are restricting your new body that is trying desperately to emerge. A good portion of the battle is always your attitude and belief.

When we begin to <u>believe</u> that the Universe is full of infinite possibilities we can move beyond our limits. If we do so, we will begin to experience phenomenal occurrences within our life. We may begin meeting the people we have been wanting to meet. We may find ourself living in circumstances that we have always dreamt about living. We may find situations in our life seemingly falling into place. We will even learn new things about ourself and others. This is not to say that once we begin to open to the world of limitless possibilities that our life becomes easy and effortless. This is not the case. The irony is that circumstances seem to move quicker and faster while we are in the midst of creating possibilities and making connections, yet we still experience life as we previously had with all of its ups and downs. However, we come to experience life with a new level of understanding. This new understanding helps us to see, acknowledge, and honor how all of these occurrences and events within our life have specific interconnecting purposes resulting from our choice to expand our beliefs and thus, expand our experiences with the creative flow.

Our soul, our spirit, wants evolution and growth. It knows that

49

it is of limitless form, therefore, it knows limitless thought. It is patient with us while we strive to control, manipulate, analyze, and contain everything about our life. It wants us to experience our life in our own way, but it also wants us to know its world of limitless expression. The soul knows that life is lived for the purpose of evolution and growth. This includes encountering a full expression of who we truly are. We move closer and closer to this full manifestation of ourself when we journey along the path of moving beyond our limits.

ALL VIEWS ARE CORRECT

All views are correct. To hold a single point of view does not mean that your view must be right and therefore, the opposite view must be wrong. Both viewpoints are "right" in their own way. They are both worthy viewpoints relative to the person, the situation, or the circumstance at hand.

Our views are determined by our collective background. This background is comprised from our beliefs, heritage, cultural and environmental influences, and personality, to name a few. This makeup influences the kinds of views we will hold. There is nothing wrong with having a view or an opinion. However, it becomes troublesome when we begin to believe that our view and our opinion is the correct answer and, for that matter, the only answer. When we believe this, we shut out other possibilities, thus, limit ourself. We keep ourself from learning about new viewpoints and growing to new heights. Everyone has their own perspective on things and that doesn't make anyone wrong for holding their own personal perspective. It just means that each individual has determined his/her own personal structure for viewing and understanding the world. How can we discount anyone's attempts for trying to do this? Our views, our perceptions, are what allow us to understand our world because they give us a framework in which to experience the world.

When we do clutch to a view, as if this view was written in stone, we do so at the expense of losing the opportunity to explore and expand into new arenas and travel down new avenues. For example, we drive a certain way commuting to and from work and have come to believe that this way is the best way to travel. It is believed to be the best way to go. Another individual has another route to take. Now, if we are not open to hearing about it and possibly trying this different route, ourself, we will probably never experience this other possibility. Maybe, at some point in time, the other route is tried and we come to learn that this way is even less congested with traffic and even more scenic than our original way. We can only discover a new route, a new way, when we are open to experimenting and suggestions. Being free of judgment toward others' points of view provides us ample opportunities to continually experience a newness in life. Think of the old saying, "Never judge a man without first having walked a mile in his shoes." Remember, when we judge others' perceptions as wrong, we lose the opportunity to travel many miles on new and different routes.

When we allow ourself to look at things from another perspective, from someone else's eyes, we allow ourself to grow and expand. We allow ourself to learn about the acceptance of others, including ourself. The world becomes a place of exploration, a world of newness and of uncharted territories, expanding into infinite possibilities.

When we regard our point of view as correct and as being the right way, by default we are saying that another way, differing from our way, must be wrong. All views are just different views, neither right nor wrong, but just varying ways different individuals perceive and interact within their environments. So, in this manner all views are correct and exist to help us make independent sense of our existence.

We may think that our way of doing something is the best way, the right way, or the only way. If we open our eyes we'll see that another is just as adamant about his/her way of doing something. We ask ourself, how can two ways of doing something or two different points of view both be the best way or the right way? It is readily answered by the wise words of a spiritual master, "All paths lead to the top of the mountain." We have all just found different paths through varying experiences and perspectives. We can learn from each other when we forego the judgment.

It is important for us to understand this principle of "all views are correct." As we do so, it helps us remain open to the field of all possibilities. It helps us remain open to our creative heritage. It helps us connect with others, incorporate, and integrate new concepts. This means that we don't live in a vacuum and we don't have to reinvent the wheel. We can build upon others' perspectives and views, allowing these ideas to change as they need to. We harbor controlling agendas when we believe our view is the only way or another's viewpoint is wrong. We manipulate and negate the other individual's perceptions when we deem his/her perspective as wrong. We control the other individual's experiences when we believe that our way is the way things should be done, viewed, and approached. Controlling behaviors foster a degree of "stuckness" in life that prevents growth. We may not agree with another individual's point of view, but nevertheless, this view belongs to this individual and is important to him/her for understanding the world. We don't have to accept nor adhere to another person's point of view or perspective, but by being open to these different perceptions, we learn about unlimited thinking and choice. Developing and nurturing this type of attitude helps us become less egotistical, prejudicial, racial, bigoted, and separative. Another person's point of view and another group's perspective might not be for you, but it is for them. This needs to be accepted. When we do this we help others begin to accept beliefs and views that are different from their own. We help them accept us. We help ourself and, consequently, help others to accept the subtle nuances and maybe even learn to appreciate the major differences. This type of thinking and approach can help bring people together and move mountains.

Chapter 4 - CREATIVE DUALISM

When it comes to understanding the legacy of our magnificent energy, known as creativity, we come to learn that we embody an incredible strength. This inner strength, this creative energy, cannot be fully expressed if we are saying one thing and doing another or being bombarded by outside pressure to be one way when, internally, we feel differently. The channel for creativity's expression flows from authenticity. In other words, being honest with ourself and recreating this honesty outwardly promotes the flow of creativity. Not only must we secure an honest dialogue with ourself, but we must come to terms with the inevitable flux of inner growth. Growth stems from change of some sort or another. An upheaval to our existence results when the element of change is introduced. Many of us fight change since we must revise our life and incorporate the change into our present existence. This means being, doing, or having things differently. With growth, not only our outer life changes, but our inner world is effected too. Change is not what creates the turmoil. It is our resistance to the change that brings the turmoil and the pain.

When change meets our existing life head-on, the manifestation of uncertainty results. Change catapults us into a new direction or into the crossroads. It is being at the crossroads or at the place of uncertainty this chapter addresses (more about change in chapter 5). The importance of not rushing this uncertain time, and instead learning to channel the resulting ambiguity and anxiety, needs to be explored. There is energy, incredible energy, living within our trying times.

At some time or another, all of us have struggled with tension within our life. Tension leaves us existing in an in-between place, the purgatory of life. Sometimes it feels as if we will reside there indefinitely. Tension occurs when we, as human beings, change and evolve. Evolution depends upon the principle of tension. When we simultaneously hear the collective, ideological "shoulds" coming at us in one ear and our own inner voice coming to us in the other ear, we find ourself, in many cases, within the tension between opposite thinking. This is limbo. The typical response is to feel stuck and despondent. However, the tension we feel serves as a barometer measuring the struggle between the pressure of external demands and our presenting inner needs. We can view the tension as a sign of friction, igniting change in our life where it is needed. We respond to this friction in many ways. Our unconscious awareness of these opposing forces strives for balance. Our psychic makeup strives for a sense of equilibrium in the midst of imposing conflict. We gain consciousness as we are confronted by the seemingly incongruous opposites that crucify us. We question whether or not and/or how we can stomach these presenting opposites, the resulting tension and friction, within our life any longer.

If we can learn to exist in the in-between space, that limbo, where we take in both points of views and beliefs, we then allow a balancing feat to occur that can promote our own kind of blending to emerge. An answer, a direction, a solution, can be produced when we hold both points of view together, transcending each of their extremes, yet blending something from each. This is much like offspring of parents, a part of each, yet beyond the original forms. We can learn to develop and evolve into the unique individuals that we are. We are continually asked to explore the areas of gray within our life. Opposite views that exist together stir up tension and turmoil, even if we are not consciously aware of them. Bringing consciousness to these conflicting views helps us work with the resulting tension through cognitive awareness. Being aware allows us to focus the flow of our creative energy. This energy helps us evolve. The tension between opposite influences, becomes the channel, the vessel, the energy source, that we can use to journey inward and discover the authentic and evolving true Self. We tend to find meaning within our life through the tension and the struggle.

Going into these places of dualism, this tension, requires courage. Courage is needed for creativity to thrive. The courage to take risks, have patience, listen inwardly, feel uncomfortable, is necessary for our creative essence to be discovered and engaged. This means that we can be with our inner world with all of its experiences intact and not need to escape it or suppress it. This takes courage and leads us to the creative life.

Tension is the area between chaos and order. It is that space between opposites. Tension is a component of what it means to be alive and conscious. When we feel tension, we are reminded of our own humanness, how it feels to be alive, feel emotions, and experience situations. All of these events bring real feelings. The internal, evolutionary tension we experience brings us back into our awareness of life. Tension keeps us conscious and creative.

When we explore the concept of creative dualism more, you might find it helpful to have a visual image in mind. An image for creative dualism is the SUN and the MOON. Envision the importance of both the sun and the moon.   The gravitational pull of the moon influences the watery tides of the oceans and possibly, our seas of emotions. The fiery sun provides life. Both provide light, but in different ways. The sun is its own burning source of light, while the moon reflects the sun, exuding a glowing essence. Sometimes, on a clear day you will see both inhabiting the sky, sharing this space. The concept of dualism that is being explored here is much like the sun and moon, both aspects sharing the same space, but each having a different purpose. It's important to recognize this as we delve further into the presence of creative energy and its dualistic nature.

CREATIVITY AND CHAOS

Many times, being open to the creative process within our life forces us to give up control. Chris Griscom, in her book, The Healing of Emotion, reminds us that "Often it is only when we give up ego control that the unmanifest can come forth and be manifest[ed] in a new, more beautiful, miraculous, and enlightened way." However, quite often the process of relinquishing control can feel like we are existing within an absolute state of chaos, total discord. At other times it makes us feel vulnerable. Creative energy is born from out of these times. We need to understand how to channel the chaotic energy and engage it as constructive creative energy instead of feeding its usual downhill course of destructiveness. We must also learn to let go when needed.

Chaos, total disorder, sends us spiraling down and whirling in circles. When areas within our life feel chaotic we feel out of control and at the mercy of this unpredictable amusement park ride. Yet, there is nothing amusing about this ride. Chaos within our life tends to breed more chaos as we seemingly become pawns to her whim. Chaos becomes something we would rather do without. Banish the chaos! Should we or can we even do this?

In various mythologies of antiquity, Chaos is the formless darkness, the beginning of creation. She gives birth to form, thus bringing forth life. She embodies creation. Her mythology provides us a powerful metaphor for understanding chaos within our life. Somewhere in the womb of total disorder is a seed of newness just waiting to develop and be born. If in the midst of chaotic feelings we can honor these pangs of chaos as an initiation into a new life, then chaos becomes an ally. Not that feeling chaotic or being surrounded by chaos is a pleasant and memorable experience. To the contrary, we tend to feel hopeless, helpless, and hapless. These feelings become the fuel that chaos continually feeds upon. It's important that we don't get stuck in these feelings concerning our chaotic situation. Becoming stuck in the chaos means that we see no light at the end of the tunnel and no way out. Our Inner Self knows that pain created by chaos is short and equivocal, but our human Self identifies with the chaos and suffers. Engaging with chaos in this manner creates an inner despondency that sets us up for destructive creation.

Destructive creativity is about bringing forth to our life what we do not want. When we are stuck in feelings of dejection and hopelessness we tend to ruminate over our situation. The continual dwelling in our chaotic plight becomes a source of virulent energy attracting more destructiveness to us. This becomes a vicious cycle and we find ourself buried in the chaos. We must find a way to counteract the destructive momentum.

By being conscious of this destructive pattern, we bring awareness to the situation. It is important to honor the change, disguised as chaos, that will inevitably bring us into newness. It is important to remember that it is not the world outside of us that brings us into disorder, but our inner world of struggle that does. We struggle as we attempt to escape the chaos by means of covering it up and/or suppressing it. We struggle as we resign ourself to our "unlucky" and unhappy predicaments. Instead, we must face Chaos by comprehending her power, realizing our weaknesses, and honoring the change she bestows on us. With this understanding we emerge from her grasp by channeling her energy through our awareness of her clandestine intents. We learn to work in unison.

HOW DO I CHANNEL CHAOS CREATIVELY?

Before we begin with the following exercise, it is important that I explain what is involved with any therapeutic art exercise. I am going to tell you the same thing I have been telling all of my art therapy participants for years. What I am going to ask you to do does not require any artistic flair or background. All this exercise asks of you is for your self-expression in whatever way it happens to emerge. There is no right or wrong way of doing this. Just trust your own way as "the way" it needs to be done. Please try to suspend criticism and judgment and allow self-expression.

Directions -

Expressing Chaos

In your mind's eye picture the chaos that you are currently

experiencing. Notice how it makes you feel. Be aware of any related colors. Feel any movement associated with it. What symbol or symbols would represent the tension you feel. Trust anything that comes to mind.

Now, use pictures either drawn, painted, and/or cut out from magazines to express and allow the chaos to have form on paper. Take your time letting yourself graphically face the chaos. Trust your own process, creating as many images as you need to allow chaos its full expression. Right now you are not trying to hide or escape from it. You are trying to learn from it. Let it express. When you feel complete with this process, look at your image(s) in succession. Be open to what it may be conveying to you. Ask your artwork, I repeat, <u>ask your artwork</u> (meaning, any creation you have expressed) the following questions. Write the answers you receive on paper or even on the artwork itself.

How does it feel to express yourself?

How does it feel to look the way you do?

What do you want to say now that I'm listening?

What do you want to show me?

What can I learn from you?

How can I learn from you?

What newness are you giving birth to?

What is dying off?

How can we work together?

(And any other question you would like to ask it).

I know that this may seem silly and may require you to be alone with your image(s) to do this, but stick with it and you may be surprised with the responses your artwork has to offer you.

CREATIVITY AND TENSION

Where there is tension, there is creativity. Creativity comes from out of this place of tension. Tension is that place of uneasiness in which we struggle with the uncertainty of the experience. We, humans, tend to resist change unless it comes easily, effortlessly, and without tension. However, when we change, we grow. When we grow, we evolve. The resulting uneasiness is just part of the process. These feelings of uneasiness can come or develop out of many different situations. We know when we are in this place of tension because we tend to have a hard time making up our minds, we feel uncomfortable, desperate, and we want to rush through the experience and the situation. We tend to sense a feeling of impatience and a sense of anxiety. Yet, within this space, where we would like to "hurry up" and rush through the tense experience just to "get it over with," is where the growth-producing tension resides. This place where tension exists is the place where we feel uneasy and uncomfortable. Even though most of us have been in this space at many times during our life, for the most part, it is uncharted territory. When we experience the tension, we do all that we can do to get out of it, therefore, we don't come to know this place of potential empowerment. Carl Gustav Jung, a famous Austrian psychiatrist of the 20th century, talks about this tension. He explores it by explaining the experience of two polar opposites (opposing views) existing at the same time within an individual. These views are brought to the forefront within a person's psyche by means of internal influences. In other words, the individual's system is striving for change. Dr. Jung suggested we hold the pair of opposites together to see what new attribute would evolve.

This stance requires us to stay with the tension, stay with the feelings, be in that tense place of emotions, and allow what wants to develop and emerge on its own conation. We are asked to be in that space where we must let go, allow change, and trust ourself to take the risk of being uncomfortable. If we push this process by control or manipulation we do so at the expense of aborting the powerful creative energy, the "newness," that strives to evolve. We don't want to prematurely remove ourself from this creative tension, from this place of light, and from the new creation. An example of this delicate process is illustrated by the relationship between the filament and the pair of "lead-in" wires in a light bulb. We all know how powerful, yet how fragile, the filament in a light bulb is. When a light bulb is handled carefully and not dropped, the filament remains in place mounted between the two lead-in wires. These wires support the filament and channel the current of electricity into it. The filament is what lights up. In a similar fashion, the pair of opposites (the lead-in wires) channeling the tension (the energy) supports the emergence of a new attribute (the light). Care must be provided to sustain and to not disconnect this tension so creative energy can be channeled between the two opposites.

When the pair of opposites are held together, a newness emerges; a third entity evolves. This third entity is a composite of the two opposites that came together, but it is also a distinctly new creation. This is change, this is newness, this is where creativity exists. This is creation. To be ourself, to dance our own dance, requires a will and desire to go outside and beyond the beliefs of the populace, the collective influence. Doing this creates tension between what is true to ourself and what is expected by the collective influences. Generally, to be truly oneself generates friction and tension. "This friction between opposites is the creative force of nature, and therefore, of *our* nature as well," according to Jacquelyn Small in her book Embodying Spirit. This tension can become the vehicle propelling us along our quest of finding meaning and creativity within our life.

We can think about it in terms of a male and female coming together, uniting in sexual union for the purpose of creating new life. Thus, out of the two opposites, out of the spermatozoa and the ovum, a new entity evolves, a new creation, a birth. Our own processes in life work very much in the same manner. We are bringing together conflicting parts inside of ourself and allowing these opposites to mate, create a union, and give birth to a third entity which becomes the new idea, the new situation, the change, and the creation

When we are experiencing an emotional situation that leaves us feeling uncomfortable and uneasy, maybe it's time to allow ourself to just exist within that situation. This does not mean being a glutton for punishment but it does mean trying to be with the feeling, not trying to "fix" anything, and avoiding the urge to rush through it. It is when we are within this uneasy situation in which things are tense and intense that we are at the stage of birthing pain and are preparing to deliver. A birth takes time. We are constantly conceiving and delivering new ideas, new concepts, and changes within our life. The uneasiness that is felt, that is sensed, that is known, from this tension is an important ingredient for the alchemical boiling pot that initiates the change that is about to occur. Without these uncomfortable moments and intense times, the depth of our growth and evolution can't happen. Friction is needed for fire. Tension is needed for creativity. This tension, this friction, creates a spark which helps light us on our way. The light that results can illuminate new attitudes and new beliefs that can encourage new understandings. We can learn to be in contact with who we are deep down at our core. This experience keeps us in touch with our soul and attuned to our purpose for being embodied.

As our body was growing, many of us can remember the literal pains we felt in our body as it was developing. I recall having pains in my legs which I later learned were growing pains. These were uncomfortable, but at the same time they were a necessary part of life in order to change and develop into the more mature body I was beginning to inhabit. Sometimes, pain is part of the growth and development process. If we can view the pain that tension brings as a vital element to our growth, we can learn not to fight the process of these necessary changes. This is not about advocating for pain, but it is about working with the pain inherent in life. Tension is a part of life.

From personal experience, in order for me to create a piece of artwork there has to be a desire, an inner wanting, to express and let ideas and thoughts come forth. Along with this inner desire comes the doubts, the inhibitions, the struggles, the belief, the excitement, and the impetus. All of these different feelings are coming at the same time. On many occasions, the emotions felt are conflicting. This onslaught of feelings, including all of the conflicting feelings, is the energy. That is the energy many artists use to propel their creative endeavors forth. This energy, this flow of feelings, this intense time, is what gives birth to color, form, shape, and movement to artwork. Personally, when I artistically create, the more excited I get, the more energy I have and this brings me the freedom to emit the form, the shape, and the movement that is trying to express itself from within me. I offer it permission to reveal itself. It's like giving birth to a new expression. It's like giving birth to something that is separate, yet at the same time "of" the artist. However, it has a life of its own.

Tension is the friction. It is the catalytic experience. Tension brings life to the soul. If understood, it brings us to a more conscious experience of our soul. If misunderstood, it aborts any meaningful experience or communication being extended from the soul at the time.

Yes, tension creates an uneasy, unsteady, inner force that churns and moves from within. When we don't fully understand it and if we don't fully work with it, tension becomes the lost and misunderstood inner cry. If we can begin to understand the purpose of tension within our life, we can begin to understand our own inner spark, our own inner burning passion, to express who we are inwardly and outwardly. Creativity and creation live amongst and amidst the tension, desiring to express itself in whatever form, in whatever manner, and in whatever way the individual feels is his/her own. We need not feel surprised when we feel an emotional unrest. By noticing when this is happening, we can learn to be with this tension and begin to understand what it's about. This emotional unrest can lead us directly to the foundation of ourself if we take the uneasiness in and allow ourself to hear its message. This message is fuel for the expression of our creative core. This is food for our growth. Nurture the tension as a midwife would nurture the mother during delivery. Be patient with yourself and allow the birthing process to take place. Creativity is who we are at our core. We are all creative beings and we all desperately strive and desire to be expressed, released, and heard. So be with the tension and know that you are in the wake of an incredible energy, churning and developing inside. Know that all of Creation is in awe of this incredible power and awaits your new birth.

HOW DO I WORK WITH THE TENSION?

Before we experience the related exercise, let's explore the concept with which we will be working. From medieval Christianity comes the symbol of the mandorla. The word sounds and appears similar to the word mandala, which in Sanskrit literally means circle and center. The circular shape of the mandala has been used throughout the ages in many different cultures to symbolically represent wholeness within and an interconnection with All-That-Is. The mandala is regarded as a symbol of healing. The mandorla has healing effects too, but differs in its form. The mandorla is the third shape, the almond shape, created when two circles partially overlap. It is this zone of intersection that contains a part of each circle. It is the subset we learned about in elementary math class that is created when two different groupings overlap. The mandorla teaches us that when two different aspects, including aspects that are diametrically opposed, come together, what results is a merging of the two, creating a new entity. What a powerful image to help explore the creative dualism within our life!

Directions -

Mandorla Art

Remember the suggestions given earlier in this chapter for doing any type of therapeutic art exercise. Most importantly, trust your own process.

Bring to mind two opposing issues or views within your life that seem to keep you in the middle, stuck in the tension between them. What are these diametrically opposed issues? What symbols or shapes come to mind when you think about them? Hold their images in your mind while on a sheet of paper you draw two overlapping circles, creating a mandorla. Now, using art media (such as, markers, crayons, or paints), visually express your opposing issues, one in each of the circles, paying attention to how they want to merge with each other when they both exist in the in-between space known as the mandorla. Trust what wants to happen.

When you feel complete with this exercise, spend a few moments viewing the total image. What do you notice? What happened in the overlapping space? How would it feel to be in that space? What does your picture say to you about where things stand? Write down the answers to these questions and any other things you notice. Note that this process of working with the mandorla should be repeated as long as the tension between opposites exists. The idea is not to get rid of the tension, but to channel the tension through a creative act to gain awareness and insight. Honor the tension and what it presents. When we honor the existence of opposites within our life we accept all expressions of ourself. This is important for developing the full expression of our creative essence. This brings us in contact with the richness of life. As Matthew Fox, a post-modern theologian and author, says, "We learn we are cosmic beings not only in our joy and ecstasy, but also in our pain and sorrow." The level of experiencing heartfelt internal, blissful joy in our life is proportional to the level we allow ourself to experience the dark night of the soul. They appear to be opposites and diametrically opposed experiences, but in actuality, they come from out of the same place. They are part of the same mandorla.

Chapter 5 - CREATIVE EMPOWERMENT

Experiencing the power of creativity involves accepting the processes of change. Change promotes empowerment, transformation, and liberation within our life. Empowerment is derived from owning and accepting the transforming elements of change. This element is energy, pure creative energy that brings us new experiences and offers us growth. When we begin to own and accept ourself for "who we are," including all of the adjustments we have endured, we embark on a powerful journey of transformation. By accepting this principle of change, we open ourself up to the procurement of our "wonders." These wonders include all of our inner abilities we may or may not be aware of. We begin to feel empowered. We begin to feel transformed and liberated by these recognitions we are having about ourself. This awareness stems from the freedom that occurs when we begin to understand that we are creative beings and hold in our hearts the ability to co-create our world, our life, through the changes we brave, the thoughts we hold, and the choices we make.

INCREASE PERSONAL EMPOWERMENT
Accepting ourself is the key to personal empowerment. This means accepting our imperfections, shortcomings, and weaknesses. This also means accepting our personal power, the abilities, potentials,

and strengths we enshroud. Believe it or not, our abilities are even harder for many of us to accept. Most of us are really good at picking ourself apart and being all too aware of our downfalls and flaws, as we aren't typically this focused on our capabilities. We tend to identify with the nature of ourself we dislike the most because that is what we tend to perseverate on. By doing so, we cut ourself off from all other possibilities that do exist within us. We restrain ourself from true empowerment.

However, self-acceptance does not mean a bitter-sweet resignation to a "messed-up" life. It does not mean using it as an excuse to avoid change, growth, and development. Becoming more accepting of yourself does mean understanding that you have done all that you could possibly do giving everything you believed and knew at any specific time in your life. It's about being open to the fact that maybe you have made choices that you later came to regret, but at the time, they <u>were</u> the choices available and the choices to be made. Would you do things differently now? Probably. Maybe. And if we had done things differently back then, we would be in a dynamically different situation right now. We might even be a different personal all together, for better or worse. But, there is no way to really know. Hindsight is always 20/20. Having compassion and understanding with ourself and with others in the here and now evokes personal empowerment. We must learn to be self-forgiving.

When we own an earnest desire to "better" ourself, it becomes easier to accept the nature of ourself in the here and now. With this sincere desire we open ourself to all of our latent possibilities. When we do so, we increase our ability to deal with the shortcomings of our actual Self, as compared with our ideal Self, because we understand that we are on a path of learning and growth. We know that life is about perfecting our development. We become compassionate and empathic toward our path and the path of others. In the end, we realize that only the individual has jurisdiction over who he/she is. We accept responsibility for our life and the quality of it. We accept responsibility for where we have been and where we are going.

When we explore ways throughout this chapter to increase personal empowerment, you might find it helpful to work with a visual image. A potent image for empowerment is a TORCH. Imagine an incredible, brightly burning torch lighting your way. You hold it with dignity and respect, much like the Statue of Liberty does, for you know that your empowerment represents freedom to you. Feeling empowered unlocks the dam and unleashes the flowing waves of creative energy. Creative energy is our freedom.

CREATIVITY AND CHANGE
Creativity comes out of experimentation. Experimentation is merely trial and error, trying out new ideas, new concepts, attempting something a different way, and then adjusting ourself to the

transformation of the outcome. This whole process can be summed up in one word: change.

The concepts of change and creativity are closely related. Creativity is that place of knowing, that place of being, that allows us to express who we are and what we are about. Change is the avenue in which our creative spark and interests develop. Without change there would be no new developments and investigations nor would there be creative spurts of growth. Change is that constant agent that provides us with the environment to foster our creative growth. Change and its power of transformation is an inevitable process. If there is one thing we can count on, it is change. Since we will all experience this process we had better learn to work with it, not against it.

Many of us fight change and hate change. We hate it because we fear it. When we fight and fear change, we experience our growth as being laborious and difficult. We will experience chaos and agitation. We will create what we fear. Change catapults us into the unknown. Change pushes us out of our comfort zones and into new, uncharted territory. This tends to cause anxiety, confusion, and overwhelming feelings. These feelings are "rightly so" reactions to our changing experiences. These feelings mark our initiation into the throes of change. However, when we are forced to go beyond our comfort zones, we widen our boundaries and expand our horizons. The discomfort we feel escorts us into the experience of new and different things. As we all know, these experiences generally aren't always pleasant at the onset of change, but these experiences aren't always unpleasant in the end. Change is an invitation into new experiences. It is the gate keeper of uncharted territory. When we learn to embrace change and its seemingly impulsive untimeliness, we learn to be more spontaneous with life. We learn to go with the flow. We learn to meet events head on. We become stronger in character and truer to our faith in ourself.

When we are asked to go beyond our usual way of thinking, being, acting, knowing, seeing, feeling, and sensing, we are being cosmically pushed to expand ourself. When we must experience new things, we open the door to new possibilities. We step through the doorway and find ourself in a new situation. Maybe we have experienced similar situations, but not one with the exact circumstances that are happening in this exact same manner. Therefore, we experience a creative challenge. We are called upon to learn and to grow. We are being challenged to respond. We access the situation and experiment with our response(s). Some responses may be productive and constructive; others may be destructive. We respond and we learn from both.

We are confronted with possibilities and an infinite number of ways we can respond. Life encourages us to move beyond our comfort zones and experience different things. Change fuels our creativity. Doing the same things over and over again, repeating a routine, and living life in check, causes our creative energy to become stifled, stuck, and stagnant. Our soul magnetizes challenging events to us in order to get things moving again. Being alive is not about being complacent. We are alive to move, to change, to be, and to create. Our creativity needs freshness and newness. It needs change.

Change is that element that puts the "life" in living. It is the action part of being alive. It allows everything around us to come to life whether this means feeling intense feelings, experiencing new ways of responding, thinking new thoughts and ideas, or physically and mentally being in a new space of unknown and uncharted territories. Change can push us into the unknown and mysterious regions of ourself. As Deepak Chopra, a leading endocrinologist and best-selling author, says, "When something seems to change in the world...it is really you that is changing." Change helps us become acquainted with strengths we never knew we had. When we experience change we access new dimensions of ourself.

If a creative person in our society is someone we deem as being spontaneous, experimental, inventive, and artistic, then this is because this creative person knows how to work with change. The works of this "supposed" creative person are able to reflect the continually changing different moods, different dimensions, and different environments that are a part of this person's experiences. The soul of the individual is exposed upon the canvas of life. My work as an art therapist has shown

77

me that by being attentive to an other's artwork and observing this creator at work with his/her own personal process, there is a lot that can be learned about this individual.

Change exposes all of our souls. Change thrusts us into knowing ourself. This may be the reason why many of us fight change. After all, change makes us think about things, such as who we are, where we are going, and what we are about. It requests we live the self-examined life. According to the Greek philosopher Plato, "The life which is unexamined is not worth living." When we are pushed to look at ourself, we begin to examine who we are. This process of examination makes us feel vulnerable because it exposes ourself. When change occurs it breaks down the safe structure and routine we have become so accustomed to. Our fortress, as we have known it, dissolves along with our comfortable parameters of safe living. We transform and change similar to the snake who outgrows his skin and sheds it quite naturally. We shed our personas, the masks we wear, and the roles we play. We even shed environments, habits, and friends which no longer support our new way of being. We continually go through the stages of being a chrysalis protected by its cocoon, transforming into the butterfly ready to spread its wings and fly. We know this process. We are aware of its recurrence and hence, our renewal.

Each time, change requires us to develop new protocols and paradigms from which we must respond. With each newly established structure, inevitable change continually challenges our comfort zones. In this growing process we become quite creative with responding to these changes. Change shakes us up and we pick up the pieces, but in a different way each time.

POWER OF THE PRESENT

The present is where our empowerment resides. By being fully focused in the present we tap into our space of personal empowerment. It is within the present where we can live freely and authentically because in the present we are living without the baggage of the past and the worries for the future. This entails being focused in the here and now, being fully alive in the present moment. It means living as if every moment counts, because in fact, every moment does. We often forget this concept as we plan, worry, and sweat over the future. In the meantime, our life is ticking away. When we worry about the future or fret over the past, we forego our freedom for making clear choices because we tend to make choices blemished by what we fret over and worry about. We become imprisoned by our past and bound by our future.

The energy and power of the Universe is in the present. This is the gift the Universe bestows on us. What we are thinking, whether it be related to the past, present, or future, the Universe interprets it as occurring in the present. This is how our past can haunt us and our future can enslave us. There is no sense of time for the Universe. Time

79

is a man-made structure to quantify our existence and provide us the arena to witness the consequences of our choices. It allows us to view our life as a continual progression. Tomorrow and yesterday, the future and the past, are merely concepts helping us explain the passage of man-made linear time. It is our way to mark this movement.

When we are disquiet about our past we are bringing that energy into our conscious awareness, into the present moment. When we are worrying about our future, we are doing the same. All of our thoughts, regardless of their origin, occur in present time to the energy of the Universe. As the late Dale Carnegie, public speaker, educator, and author said, "The biggest lesson I have learned is the stupendous importance of what we think. If I knew what you think, I would know what you are, for your thoughts make you what you are. By changing our thoughts, we can change our lives." The thoughts we maintain about ourself, the thoughts we bring into our daily interactions, create and distinguish who we are. The thoughts, worries, disgusts, regrets, and disappointments over the past and for the future that we cling to make us who we are. So, in other words, we are bound by our thoughts, we are bound by our feelings and emotions, and we are bound by our intentions. Our thoughts, feelings, and intentions can be our personal prison or our own freedom.

When we hold tight to the baggage of the past, we do so at the expense of giving up our present opportunity to live authentically and freely. When we hold on to the past, we are colored and tainted by its grip over us. It often becomes overwhelming and entraps us. When we live for the future, we forego the opportunity to enjoy our life thoroughly as it sneaks by while we are making distant plans. When we truly live in the present, we allow all of our faculties to be focused in the moment. This allows us to be consciously aware of ourself, of others, and of our relationship with our environment. This brings great personal freedom and the ability to make untainted choices when we maintain our focus on the present moment, releasing yesterday and tomorrow. We can live our life empowered by the present.

Now, this does not mean that we must forget the past for it is important to know who we are, from where we came, and what we are about. The past has helped shape us into who we are today. In a similar light, this does not mean that we ignore our future. It is important to plan for our future, such as for our home, for retirement, and for our children's education. However, to be aware of and plan for these things does not mean that we become fixated in the past or on the future. We can do so by living in the present while paying attention to these concepts and events as needed.

The past that most of us hold tight to relates to the past pains, the unpleasant situations, and our regrets. These are the concepts that tend to tie us up, pull us down, and become baggage weighing heavily on our heart, soul, and back. Worrying about the future causes excessive planning and focusing on tomorrow while forgetting to live today. As the late rock star, John Lennon, said, "Life is what happens while we're busy making plans." By the time we finally realize that we are in the today, portions of our life have already slipped by.

When we exist within the present, we tend to feel less pain, less remorse, and less sorrow associated with the past and less worries, concerns, and anxiety over the future. It is when we hold tight to the past that we tend to experience continuously the disappointments, the failures, and the pains as if they are still happening right now. These experiences may have occurred many years ago, but the Universe views our present thoughts as our current reality. When we live our life for the future and the golden carrot eludes us, we worry whether or not we'll ever obtain it. As a result, we learn to view the world within the confines of these experiences, within the framework of these feelings, from the past and for the future.

We can determine a person's thoughts about him/herself by looking at his/her present situation. What a person thought, felt, and intended yesterday, makes the person of today. What a person thinks about him/herself today creates the person of tomorrow. Our only true place of empowerment is being focused in the present, thinking the thoughts, releasing our stored emotions, and creating the intentions in the here and now. This will take us out of yesterday, away from tomorrow, and back into today.

I repeat a little saying to myself that came to me many years ago as a young teenager. This saying has remained with me over the years. It goes like this, "Tomorrow never comes for tomorrow is always today." I say that to myself at times of procrastination as a sort of motivation to take action in the now. It works because consciously I understand that the concept of "tomorrow" is merely a label denoting the passage of time that I will never reach. I know that the true place of action is always in the present, in the here and now. When we reach tomorrow, what day is it? Well, it is today! So, in fact, we really never reach tomorrow just like we can't reach yesterday. We can think about yesteryear and next year, but in actuality, to physically be in these concepts of time are unattainable because when we are there, they become the present. I and you and everyone else is always in the today. Where we can take action and make a difference is today, in the present.

Does a passage of time ever really occur? The answer to that question would have to be "yes," but the passage of time is a physical construct not of the universal order. We do observe physical changes in our bodies, in the changing of the seasons, in the erosion of our roads, and in the cost of living. Things are changing and the concept of time marks the passing of these changes. Yet, the only place where we have the ability to experience these changes is in the present.

Being of the physical is just one order of the many experiences comprising our soul. Our soul knows timelessness. In the physical, human existence we do experience a passage of time regardless of the timelessness of the Universe. However, we can and many of us do tap into these timeless realms of the Universe. Altered states of awareness induce the perception of timelessness and reminds us of the power of the present.

Regression therapists and researchers have shown us that clients can retrieve memories of the past and experience and relive them as if they are occurring in the present. They have also shown us that many clients have seen into future lives and have experienced prophetic visions. Nevertheless, the participants are interacting with all of these different realms of time within the present. With my personal experience as a regression therapist, I have witnessed many clients heal old wounds, whether they happened yesterday, earlier within this present life, or within a past incarnation. I have witnessed clients move into a future Self and work with the energy that is being presented. All of the work these clients have done has been accomplished in the present. They have met and worked with these time continuums within the present and have influenced change. This demonstrates how time is a man-made concept created to describe the passage of physical time. Yet, the power of creation, manifestation, and change is always in the present.

The power of healing is in the present. This is why all different types of therapy can work. They are focused on present day changes. Whether it be a body therapy, a form of psychotherapy, an energy therapy, a breathing therapy, or any other type of therapy, they all work with the individual in the present, addressing the presenting symptoms and causes that had originated earlier in time. The key is that they all work with and address the necessary changes within the structure of the present. The adjustments and changes are being addressed in the here and now, whether it be the client's mindset, the client's posturing and body alignment, or the client's breathing patterns.

Remove yourself from the clutches of the past and the grip of the future. Make the present your home. When we are in the present focused on the process of the present, we are allowing ourself to access the divine creator of the silence within. We are engaging this part of ourself to partake in our soul-making, to partake in creating our present reality, and to live within our presence. We are inviting health because we are focused in the present where healing can occur, and letting go of the past and releasing the future becomes priority.

The present is where our empowerment lies. The present is what the Universe knows. The present is where healing occurs and changes are made. The present holds intentions and offers results. All of this is possible as long as we release the past, relinquish the future, and live in the now by making the choice to be present.

RELEASING THE PAST

You do not have to move forward with past pains. You do not have to forget either, but there is a need to forgive ourself for the hardships and unpleasant experiences we found ourself within. The manner in which things used to be need not in any way, shape, or form define who we are today. We need to realize that we lived life back then the only way we knew how. Hindsight is great if we learn and then move on, but it is dangerous if we punish ourself and others because of it! We are always evolving. This is the natural progression of the soul. We learn and then have the opportunity to expand our knowledge and awareness by moving up, out, and beyond.

The power of awareness is always in the present. The "Now" is all there is. Focusing on the past keeps us imprisoned. It keeps us from the freedom offered by the present. Freedom is its gift; that is why we call it the present. By focusing on the past you keep yourself living the life assigned to you by others. You maintain yourself in your past regrets, hurts, and pains. You preserve the cyclic nature of your past, replaying who you used to be and not who you are today. This is too limiting. Growth becomes thwarted. You do not have to be a prisoner of your past any longer. No one should ever have to live their life this way. Take this opportunity and move forward with it. Forgive yourself for past mistakes and live in the present where the mistakes do not need to still be experienced.

However, self-forgiveness will probably be one of your greatest challenges. According to Robin Casarjian, author of the book Forgiveness, "There is often great resistance to self-forgiveness, for like any significant change, it is a death. It is dying to the habit of keeping ourselves small and unworthy, dying to shame, guilt, and self-criticism...." Without forgiveness we keep ourself stuck. With forgiveness, we allow ourself to expand into the realm of compassion and self-respect. We provide ourself with a fresh start and awaken our new birth.

HOW DO I RELEASE THE PAST?

Releasing the past is a fully cognitive and conscious process. We literally, in the physical, exist in the present even though emotionally and mentally we may still be experiencing the distress from our past. You must consciously decide that you are going to reside in the present. You must decide that you will take full responsibility for yourself and for your life. By consciously making this decision, you set the grounds for becoming your own person. You do not have to make this into a hard process, but you do have to make an open assessment of your level of self-acceptance. You can do this in many different ways, but they all require absolute honesty with yourself.

Directions -

Releasing the Past

One way to do this is to sit down, take your time, and compose a written list of all the things (situations, events, people) that keep you focused in the past. Include the so-called "mistakes" you have made, your past hurts, disappointments, and anything else you can think of. Look at each individual item and discover something new about it, for example, ask yourself what you are learning about yourself as a result. What do you regret? What would you have done differently? What self-diminishing statements would you have to release in order to forgive yourself? By acknowledging these questions you are acknowledging the insight you have gained from the situation. You are trusting your ability to know. Now, ask yourself to extend compassion to yourself for being involved in the event(s) of the past. Know the lesson it teaches you, even though you may resist the lesson. Honor these feelings and have empathy for the part of you that struggles with this. Ask yourself how you have grown as a result of this event. How has it helped you become the caring and loving individual that you are? This will require some time. It may be hard to determine this for some situations because you may still be very enmeshed with the circumstance. That is okay. In some cases these circumstances have been with us for years, maybe many years, and it may take more exploration for some than for others. The key is not how quickly you do this process, but that you start the process rolling. Use your consciousness as the key that unlocks your imprisoned Self. Bring your full awareness into the freedom of the present where you can now allow the true unfolding of your creative life. Creativity thrives on freedom.

RELINQUISHING THE FUTURE

If we live for the future, we lose sight of the present. The power of creativity lies in the present. If we continually live for the day when we have more money, become more happy, have more time, then we lose sight of our present abilities, strengths, and dreams. When we constantly worry and fret over the great unknown mystery of life, we create unnecessary hardships and chaos for ourself. Before we know it, the quality of our life has diminished.

The subconscious mind, the great manifester of realities, knows only what it currently thinks. By continually placing our life on hold while living for the future or worrying about the future when we need to be focused on the present, we abort the subconscious mind's magnetic abilities to attract these things to us in the here and now. If you live for how you want things to be in the future you will never experience it in the present. You will push the creative energy into the future and instead, experience an emptiness and a longing in the present, in the here and now. The power of creation lies only in the present moment. What we think in the now is what we will find in our future. The secret to a happy and healthy future lies in the thoughts and actions we maintain now. No need to put off our dreams anymore due to excuses.

When we take action toward them now, we fill our subconscious mind with thoughts of prospect, perseverance, and fulfillment. This is what we will inevitably draw to ourself. This becomes our current reality. This is how dreams manifest.

HOW DO I RELINQUISH THE FUTURE?
You relinquish the future once you begin to understand the principles of creativity. Creative energy flows in all places and through all things. It is energy that collects in areas where focused attention is placed. This means that an unpleasant focus can magnify unpleasant creation. This also means that a pleasant focus can draw this type of creation to us. The axiom, "like attracts like" illustrates this principle. When we worry, we draw the energy of anxiety toward us. When we live for tomorrow, we place our creative energy ahead of us. We never quite hook-up to it, therefore, we lose our ability to own who we are in the here and now. Instead, we find ourself never fully satisfied, longing and searching for something, never realizing that what we can't find is our creative empowerment. We disconnect from it in our overwhelming concern for the future. We forget to live with ourself in the present where the true energy of creative empowerment resides, where our ability to unleash our potential awaits. You can learn to become more aware of yourself in the present by taking time to "smell the roses." This means recapturing your playful spirit. Take a long walk noticing what's around you. Turn on music and move freely. Experiment with

new art materials. Use your feet to draw. Go to the park or to a sporting event. Play a game with a companion. Watch clouds create various shapes. Meditate. Pray. Have a picnic. Go splash in a pool. Do anything that encourages your spirit to play!

The idea is to experience the present by being in it. The more we consciously take time to just be in the here and now, the easier it becomes to own our creative essence and allow our creative energy to flow. The present can be a part of our workday and busy schedules too. When things are getting hectic, take a deep breath, and recapture feelings from a playful time. Remind yourself to lighten up. When we become frantic we restrict the flow of creativity and step out of our seat of empowerment. Focus on only the projects or tasks that have priority. Simplify. Remember, the present is where you have free will and can make all the difference in your life. What a wonderful gift the present is and deserves to be!

Chapter 6 - CENTERING CREATIVITY

Centering ourself within our own power heightens creativity. This empowers us to become an open conduit, channeling endless creative energy. Such an undertaking requires courage. The word *courage* originates from its Latin roots *cor* meaning *heart*, and *age* meaning *belonging to*. To have courage means to have heart, for courage belongs to the heart. When we open our heart to creative energy, compassion stirs and reminds us to courageously tend to the heart whether it is the heart of a situation, the heart of another, or the heart of broken or mending relations. Opening our heart opens us to incredible strengths and connections we might not have known otherwise.

To the heart that is open, the authentic life becomes an attainable concept. We desire to seek a sense of real balance within our life. We want to live up to the inner standards of who we really are and of who we really can be. We live this and we express this. A balance between our inner world and our outer world comes to fruition. By establishing this balance we foster a gateway between both worlds, allowing each to flow into the other. With this channel intact, we allow our creative essence to flow compassionately, inwardly and outwardly for ourself and for others. We can learn to feel centered and balanced even when life seemingly tries to knock us down.

The powerful image of the HEART can represent the concept of centering our creativity. The heart lies at the center of our own circulatory system, pumping blood and oxygen through our bodies with the flow of our breath. The heart regulates our internal flow. The heart balances and mediates between our gut reactions and our intellectual responses. Our heart is at the center of matters and at the center of our life. We must learn to center ourself and balance our life much like the regulating organ we call our heart. Our breath is the breath of our universe, of our life. Our heart supports our breath of life.

When we ignore the heart, we become negligent with ourself. We forget to take care of ourself. Our attention goes elsewhere. We lose self-care and courage. This is not to say that we must become hedonistic, this type of self-absorption is too extreme and creates an imbalance. However, it is to say that we must tend and pay attention to ourself in order for the creative energy to flow. Learn to listen to your heart. Make time for hearty activities and heartfelt pursuits. Live life with all of your heart and soul. This attention to the heart of ourself allows creativity to flow within our life. It invites breath, making room for breathing space. It invites balance.

Over a decade ago, I worked as the staff art therapist at a long-term, residential psychiatric treatment center for adolescents in Texas. A mouthful and a handful! I was always looking for interesting and creative outings to take the patients on. I had heard about a great youth educational program that Sea World of Texas was providing. I decided to call their program coordinator. I told her about our program and about my work as the center's art therapist and I requested information to be sent to my department. When the package finally arrived, it was addressed to my name along with the title, "Heart Therapist." I laughed, but also knew how appropriate that title really was. Throughout the years, I have often thought about the meaning of my renamed title. When we tend to ourself and others we are actually providing care from the heart. Let us all be heart therapists.

STRIKING BALANCE

It is extremely important to strive for balance within our life. Too much of something at the expense of forgetting about another is the same thing as being out of balance. To believe that we can constantly live a perfectly balanced life is a utopian dream and not of our current reality. However, to be in the continual process of striving for a balanced state is a realistic concept to be practiced within our life. To strive for balance is not an easy task. It is not a state of being we reach and then maintain. It is a forever-evolving process; for it is on the path of striving that we grow.

Maintaining balance means viewing the different aspects of our life as equal in importance. This refers to maintaining harmony within one's life. We become off-balanced when one area of our life receives all of the attention and focus, and the other areas of our life don't receive any. When this type of imbalance occurs, we find the other areas of our life begin to wither away and decay. We begin to feel out of touch with our life, with others, and with ourself. We must attend to the whole garden if we want our crops to grow. Lettuce tastes better when it's in a salad mixed with other vegetables. The aspects of ourself and of our life are like the different plants comprising the garden or the various vegetables comprising the salad. They all need care and attention if we want to harvest the fruits of our labor and enjoy our life.

This concept "striking balance" refers to being "in balance." This means considering everything, all parts of the whole, and being aware of all aspects of our life. To be balanced, to be in harmony, and to experience equilibrium, means that we pay attention to developing the many different facets of our life. When we do become engrossed in just one facet of ourself, we'll find that this type of imbalance will create lack in another area of our life. A lack of anything brings other limits and lacks to our life. In other words, once we have created this "black or white/all-or-nothing" type of thinking within our life, we begin to discover a void created where the forgotten aspect of our life once existed. We now have lack. The lack is created from the disinterest and lack of attention given to this aspect of ourself, our life. This one-sided view becomes a tumorous disease growing larger and larger, taking up more space within our life. Many times, we are not even aware that this is happening. We have become possessed by the disease of all-or-nothing thinking. We may only regain consciousness and find ourself awakened by this tumorous dichotomy after much pain and damage has already been done.

Let's explore an example. If we have an issue with money, we may find ourself constantly thinking about it. This issue may have seemingly developed out of our worry over not having it or not having enough. We begin to focus on the lack of money. This focus becomes obsessive. The more we look around us and become aware of our lack, the more we focus on it. The more we focus on it, the greater the lack of money there seems to be. It becomes a downward spiral as our thoughts are obsessed with money and we begin to try to do anything and everything to get money. Since we have given so much attention to it, we have given our power to it. We may become desperate and fall victim to the many "get rich" schemes out there. We have given our power away. We feel powerless in the face of money. We begin to believe that we will never have it or that we are unworthy of it and because of these beliefs, we won't! Remember, we attract to ourself that which we believe and feel. In this example, the main focus on an object, such as money, has become an obsession that has created lacks within our life. Not only do we have a literal lack of money, but we have created other lacks in the areas of our life we have neglected when we were so focused on money. We may even have plenty of money, yet still be so focused on it that we create lacks in other areas of our life as well. The more we focus on just one thing, the greater the lack of another. When lack is created, it grows. When it grows, it tends to multiply into other areas of our life. When we are just focused on the money, we are forgetting about other areas, aspects, and concerns of our life. An imbalance in our relationship to money and to our own power has been created. We have lost a sense of balance and harmony within our life. What is needed now is a refocus of our attention to the other areas in our life. We need to release our focus from the money, thereby reclaiming the power we have given it and refocus on that which has been neglected. Money is merely energy, neither positive nor negative. It is energy in balance. What we do with it and ascribe to it is how it interacts with us. Money flows best when it is an impartial energy.

Another example of how lack and imbalance plays out is in the area of work. We can become so focused on our work that we neglect other areas of our life, possibly our spouse, family, friends, health, interests, spiritual growth, or recreational time. Finally, one day, the worker wakes up and realizes that there is more to life than just work. We all know that all work and no play makes Jack a dull boy! But, just as importantly, all of anything creates lacks and limits elsewhere within our life. By the time this worker wakes up, it could be 20, 30, 50 years down the road. This is when the so-called "mid-life crisis" occurs. This is one scenario that can help contribute to it. We have created much lack in other areas of our life while being so focused on our work. We have limited ourself in our attention to and our interaction with these other areas so that we have created an imbalance, a loss of meaning. We have a crisis to quickly and impulsively recapture what it is that we have lost and neglected. We try to regain a sense of balance. We can avoid this type of shift in our life if we attend to all areas of our life now. We must address all aspects of our life, including the painful areas. If a part of ourself is neglected, it will find a way to be noticed. The manner in which it finds release is not always pleasant. So, it's important to be open to the spectrum of ourself and our life as we are constantly unfolding and enfolding.

When we become so focused on an event from the past, especially traumatic events that have caused their share of hardship, pain, regrets, anger, and other loaded and triggering emotions, we find ourself creating more imbalance. We may become so focused upon what has happened to us and who has done what, that we remain fixated in yesterday and yesteryear. This creates emotional and mental imbalances in the present. Once again, an imbalance creates lacks and limits within other areas of our life. These developing lacks and limits create a chain-reaction like the domino effect, creating even more lacks and limits within our life. It becomes an endless cycle cultivated by our unawareness and inattention to the rest of who we are. We are so focused on the past that we become frozen in time by this limited focus. We lose sight of the present. This impairs our mind, our emotional well-being, and our overall health. I am not suggesting we forget the trauma of yesterday. If we refocus our attention on the today, though, we will become proactive to and responsible for ourself in the present. We actually hurt ourself with our frozen focus on the past, which keeps us as its perpetual victim, and thus the victim of the imbalance inherent is such a rear-view look at life. We then become the creators of new lacks and limits within our life. We are the ones who become the creators of this imbalance and we are the ones who become its victims. The power of change and the strength of empowerment is always in the present. When we bring our awareness and focus back into the now, we release ourself from this imbalance created by our focused attention on the past. This means we attend to the wounds of our trauma by receiving the care required today and not by covering the pain with band-aids.

People come into our life who help us strike balance. For instance, during the time we are overwhelmed and consumed by thoughts of money, we may meet someone who is careless and carefree about their money. Or maybe this someone appears to have a lot of money. When we are working on an issue, we tend to attract others to us who can complement as well as amplify our issue(s). This enables us to see and experience our issue more clearly. We can learn from them and they can learn from us all at the same time. Life is one big balancing act! If we are aware and attuned, we will notice how and when this is happening within our life. We notice how our interactions with others allow us to view our own imbalance (issue) as if looking in a mirror. There are lessons to learn through other people's examples, through their words and through their actions, about how to deal with our obsessions, and thus, our own imbalances. The world becomes the looking glass through which we can view our imbalances and the forum for finding our balance.

FOCUSED AWARENESS

It's important that we discover ways to find our own sense of center and balance. When we do so, we take care of ourself. We promote an awareness of Self that transcends our wants and listens to our inner needs. We learn that our true, Inner Self is sacred and we learn to value our personal expression. This is possible when we honor our intuitions, our dreams, our hunches, our knowings, and our wishes. Finding ways to do this might seem impossibly difficult because our Western society tends to revere the intellectual, pragmatic type of thinking. We learn to condemn our dreams and inner wishes when the hard-core facts aren't present. We are taught that our physical experiences are paramount and the only reality. Our inner world with all its color and life doesn't pay the bills, now does it? The truth is, though, that without a balance between our inner and outer worlds, we will eventually find life pointless and meaningless, bordering on despair. Life is colorful, but only to those who are willing to explore all the shades of existence. This means involving our inner world with our everyday outer life.

There are various ways to do this, but it is important that each of us finds what works best for us. We will explore a few different techniques that I have found helpful for myself and for my clients. All of these techniques help the individual learn to discover, acknowledge, and express the inner world. They help with relaxation and the development of a forum for balance within our life. Most importantly, they help summon the flow of creativity into one's awareness and inspirit one with its energy.

Meditation, hypnosis, and art-making are a few techniques I personally use and have used in my private practice to help myself and others create more awareness, presence, and harmony within our life. All three techniques are similar practices. They all involve the individual entering into a state of focused awareness as the first step. In a state of focused awareness, the individual is present in the moment; there is no sense of time. In fact, the moment becomes timeless.

Both of the practices of meditation and hypnosis ask us to focus on our breathing and to employ various means of relaxation to help guide us into a mindful state. Both of these modalities are effective because they ask us to journey inwards, to listen and work with our own innate, healing-self. They ask us to be in touch with ourself. They teach us to be in communication with our inner world. They teach us self-responsibility for our well-being.

Creating art can be viewed as a form of active meditation, a hypnotic state, and a healthy state of dissociation. The art-making serves as a metaphor for being with our creations, being with our inner world. This means that the process of creating something allows us to be fully present in the moment to the point that we tend to tune out and not be aware of extraneous and external noises, sounds, or interruptions. We become so fully engaged in creating that we begin to find our breath deepening, being aware of only the present, and in tune with our faculties of creativity, our inner spirit. Time stands still for the passage of time is not felt. We begin to enter into a relaxed and focused state synonymous with a meditative, hypnotic, or constructive dissociative state. We become one with the moment and the moment is where we exist.

A state of focused awareness is much like an altered state. Meditative and hypnotic states are practiced to help one move into deeper levels of oneself where healing, creativity, divine wisdom, and knowledge can be accessed. Art-making is healing and can be exercised for the purpose of relaxation in addition to self-revelation.

Meditation, hypnosis, and art-making invite us into that space where we are silent. They invite us to go within. It is within this silence where we can begin to let go and release, forgive, and be in the present.

It is within this space where we can ascertain inner knowings and truths. We can learn to give our inner world equal footing with our outer life. This openness brings great rewards as it invites creative energy to inspire us and drive us. It becomes an open invitation to express ourself more fully within the world.

These focused awareness techniques empower us to remain in the present where change can make a difference. Engaging in one of these techniques or similar encounters can help us experience and participate in the process of being focused in the present where we can be responsible for our current experiences, how we choose to interact, react, and be proactive.

The following suggestions are provided to show you how meditation, hypnosis, and art-making can be implemented within your own life. These are only suggestions to be used as springboards for finding and developing your own way for attaining a state of focused awareness.

HOW DO I MEDITATE?

Meditation is the process of quieting yourself and retreating within. It is a form of centering yourself. There are various schools and thoughts about how to meditate and you may want to explore the different disciplines. However, what will be described here are ways to quiet yourself and to learn ways of letting go. Meditation is an inner process that requires the meditator just to be. So, we will explore the concept of moving into an awareness of being.

Directions -

Meditation

Find a space that is free from distractions. Turn off your phone ringer. You may want to set an alarm clock to go off after 15-20 minutes, as people tend to lose track of time. Find yourself a comfortable place to sit, as opposed to lying down which promotes sleep. You can sit in a traditional lotus position (knees bent with legs crossed) or in a chair with your feet touching the floor.

Gently close your eyes. Focus on your breathing or the beats of your heart. Follow the steady rhythm. Let it relax you. Now, let your thoughts go. I know, easier said than done! Try to imagine your thoughts as clouds floating by with the breeze, as my yoga teacher used to tell his class. Thoughts will come. This is a natural response and part of the process of learning to meditate. Notice the thoughts, but let them float on by. If you find yourself distracted or caught on one of the clouds of thought, just bring your awareness back to your breathing or heart beat. Trust this process and let it evolve at its own pace. The whole idea is to get out of the busy world of living and into the inner world of flow. Learn to get into a steady routine of meditating and try to keep it at a consistent time. This helps your body and spirit come to rely on this connection you are creating. Relaxation, a sense of well being, presence, and a connection with the flow of creative energy will come.

HOW DO I USE HYPNOSIS?

The form of hypnosis we will be exploring is one that you can do on your own. This type is known as self-hypnosis. Self-hypnosis is a very powerful tool that can be used for all kinds of healing and empowering means. It is an incredibly natural way to find a balance in your life between your inner and outer worlds and to feel more and more centered within your own creative energy. We will focus on its use primarily for relaxing, centering, accessing divine counsel, promoting healing, and facilitating the creative flow to which all of these experiences are related. But first, I must explain the concept of hypnosis.

Hypnosis is a natural state of focused awareness. It is accessed through the process of relaxation. It is a state of existence in which the conscious mind learns to let go and the subconscious mind becomes more accessible and available. One cannot get "stuck" in a state of hypnosis or be made to do something against one's will, as it is not a form of mind control. The big difference between the normal, waking state and the hypnotic state is one's brain wave patterns. In the waking state, one's brain wave pattern exists in the beta state, an alert state. In the hypnotic state, one's brain wave pattern exists in more relaxed, deeper states known as the alpha, theta,and delta states. Typically, a therapist serves as a guide to help the individual relax and reach these deeper levels of relaxation, usually through the process of breathing, imagery, and hypnotic inductions, e.g.: hand levitation, counting, focusing, and suggestions. Thus, you have the old black-and-white movie image of the hypnotist holding a swinging watch in front of someone's eyes saying, "you're getting sleepier and sleepier...." However, in the format presented, the suggestions given will be geared for self-hypnosis. The goal of hypnosis varies, but almost always, a relaxed state of being is the after effect.

Directions -

Self-hypnosis

As you would do for meditation, find yourself a space that is free from distractions. Turn off your phone ringer. You may want to set an alarm clock to go off after 20-30 minutes if you find that you tend to drift off. Find yourself a comfortable place to sit or to lie down. Hypnosis is an active form of relaxation whereas meditation is a passive form. With self-hypnosis you are thinking and sensing. With meditation you are freeing-up and letting go. So, lying down is an option if you think you will be able to stay awake. If you find yourself drifting off to sleep, then sleep is probably what you need. Yet, some hypnosis tapes are created to be used while you are drifting off to sleep. I mention this because you may want to make your own self-hypnosis tapes to be used in this manner.

Decide what your goal of this self-hypnosis session will be.

Having a goal helps you focus your intent for the session. Would you like to access divine guidance? Would you like to focus on healing energy? Would you like to magnify the flow of creative energy within your life? Have a focus for your session. This helps provide you with a structure until you feel comfortable to go within freely. There will be times when you will want a structure and times when you don't. Learn to be flexible with your own needs.

Close your eyes. Turn your attention away from your environment and onto your breath. Focus on your breathing. With each breath you take, gently allow yourself to relax. Breathe into the major parts of your body one at a time on the inhale and release any tension present in the specified place on the exhale. Take your time. (Pause.) Take slow and deliberate breaths. Once feeling relaxed, imagine an elevator, escalator, or staircase that can take you down into deeper levels of relaxation. You step into the elevator or onto the escalator or stairs and begin your downward movement. You decide how many steps your staircase has or how many floors your elevator must pass. Go down slowly until you stop. (Pause.) Once at the bottom, imagine a door that you can open. Behind the door is the specific help, answer, or guidance to the goal you had identified at the beginning of your session. A powerful helper awaits you to guide you on your way. Open the door and trust what you need to hear, see, and experience. This helper may come in any shape and size. It may just be the experience itself. Be open, trust, listen, and ask questions as you think of them. Take your time. (Pause.) When your visit is complete, thank your helper for any message imparted or wisdom bestowed. Return through the door. Slowly go up the elevator, escalator, or stairs. As you reach the top, you find your awareness coming back to your environment. Take your time. (Pause.) You focus on your breathing again. You stretch and open your eyes. Welcome back.

Take the information you gained from this experience and spend some time with it. You may want to make notes and explore it later. You may want to write it in a journal. You may want to draw it. You are encouraged to explore it further as this is how you help yourself find a balance between your inner and outer worlds. This is how you can honor your inner sanctuary. This is how you open a welcoming door to more and more of the creative energy waiting to enter your life. The more you access this inner wisdom, the more it becomes available to you.

You can curtail these hypnotic suggestions to fit your own needs. You can even make an audio tape with your own voice reading these suggestions, allowing the necessary amount of time needed to follow along. Notice that, in the exercises, I have included pauses where they would be most helpful. A tape is great because then you just pop it in and relax without having to worry about what you have to do next. Either way you do it, make sure it fits your needs.

HOW DO I INCLUDE ART-MAKING WITHIN MY LIFE?

Art-making is another process you can use to increase feelings of presence and balance within your life. It is a wonderful way to enliven your spirit and embody it with the flow of creativity. The art-making process I am discussing here is for the purpose of self-exploration and establishing a dialogue between your inner and outer worlds. Therefore, the ability to engage in this process of creating art does not require an artistic background. As I stated earlier, there is no right or wrong way for expressing yourself with art. There are merely different forms of expression and different results. Instead of focusing on what the artwork becomes, try to stay focused on what it is like for you to make and experience the specific piece of art. Stay in the present. Stay in the process.

Directions -

Art-making

Create a collection of art supplies that strike your interest. Have crayons, pastels, and markers handy. Magazines that you don't mind cutting up can be of great use. Save various odds and ends and scrap materials. Keep a supply of variously sized and colored paper. You don't need to invest a lot of money into the supplies unless you want to. It's wonderful if you can keep a box or container full of these items that can be easily accessed when needed. You will find yourself making more art if you can keep it hassle-free.

The following is a list of suggested topics to work with that can give you a starting point. Many of us need ideas until we feel more comfortable developing our own or allowing what I call "free expression" to emerge. Start with deciding upon a topic. Then without thinking too much, choose the art medium that seems to call out to you for this specific session. It might be one medium; it might be several media. Trust your feelings. Choose your paper and begin. Planning is discouraged. Let the topic move you from within and place this on the paper. Scribbles, movements, shapes, words, and images, anything goes. Suspend judgment and allow expression. Don't make something happen; just let it flow.

Topic Ideas -

Who Am I?	How does my heart feel?
My inner world	How do I feel about change?
What have I been wanting to say?	What do I need to release?
What does balance mean to me?	What is personal empowerment?
Where do I feel an imbalance?	What is creativity?
My mediation experience	My energy today
My self-hypnosis experience	Health/illness

When finished creating your image or images, take time to jot down feelings and experiences related to creating the artwork. Now, view your artwork. Place it where you can see it while literally stepping back from it. Allowing space between you and the artwork enables you to view it with objectivity. What do you notice? Remember, this is not about judging the quality of your piece. Spend a few more moments writing down what you notice. As was suggested in an earlier chapter in this book, allow your artwork to talk. This means asking your artwork questions and letting the answers come to you (refer to the section on Expressing Chaos in Chapter 4). Write these down. Any piece of artwork will continue speaking to you if you provide it the space to do so. Hang up your artwork. Live with your images. Periodically, spend time with them. Write down your responses, reactions, and thoughts. Create more artwork that comes from out of these sessions. The idea is to allow the images to live. By doing so, you are opening your conscious awareness to the internal creative energy that resides within. You are supporting a balanced interplay between your internal and external Self. This supports a ceaseless communion with creative energy.

CREATIVITY AND AUTHENTICITY

When we live our life creatively, we are allowing our authentic Self to express itself. The authentic Self is the composite of all the parts that make up who we are, our individual uniqueness. This, of course, includes the buried, the blatant, and the so-called "bad" aspects of ourself. The mythical journey we must travel to find this authentic Self is merely the journey of true expression. It is not an outward journey, but rather an inward journey for finding expression within the outer world. Living with our authentic Self does not mean that we will have blissful experiences during all moments of our life, and when we don't, this means we must have failed. Rather, it is about being fully present within our life, responding and living our soul's calling. When we live our soul's calling, we are being true to ourself. We are living the authentic life. That means we are living our life to the best of our own capabilities regardless of the popular beliefs and notions upheld by our community, society, and culture. These popular beliefs and notions that society tends to hold in reverence are known as collective views. When we bypass the collective views and learn to live out of our own heart, we invite soul to be present within our life. Where there is soul, there is creative passion brewing. We learn that we are multi-faceted pegs unable to fit into the stamped out, rounded holes invented by the standards of our society. When we try to force ourself into these prescribed holes, we have to cut off many of our facets. At the expense of doing so, we lose our unique shape, our unique expression. We become diamonds without our sparkle. Living a soulful life means experiencing life as it presents itself and as one chooses to exist within it.

Creativity and authenticity go hand in hand. To live one's life creatively means to make choices according to oneself. It means being honest with ourself and living this life as fully as possible with all facets intact. It means not having to compromise who we are at our core.

Being authentic not only means being honest with ourself, it also means being honest with others. Who I am and what you see is what you get. When we are living authentically, we cannot help but attract situations and events into our life that support this way of being. When we choose the path of authenticity we automatically begin to experience a more creatively fulfilling life.

Many of our "ills" in today's society, including but not limited to, psychological, institutional, economical, and political are partly caused by individuals replacing their soul purposes with the agendas of others', be it at work, within a family, or within a peer group. When we stifle and shut out who it is that we truly are, those parts of ourself that know and desire to do things differently from the prescribed norms, we experience these aforementioned ills. When we have a desire to express something that comes from within, a powerhouse of energy is created. This energy builds up and wants release; it wants catharsis. It wants expression. The energy can begin to take on a life of its own if not constructively and creatively directed and expressed. This is when the burning desire turns inward against ourself and becomes a self-destructing fire. This out of control fire is like an internal frustration that may go unnoticed or may be displaced outwardly. Both outcomes are destructive to the integrity of the individual. When it goes seemingly unnoticed, it doesn't stop there. It actually transforms into various emotional, mental, physical, and spiritual ailments. Eventually it creates crisis. It may become the cause of an internal emotional and mental deadening that can lead to depressed states and apathetic attitudes. It may become the cause of physical symptoms, such as tension headaches and migraines. It may become the back ache or stomach ache that apparently came about all of a sudden. Unnoticed and unexpressed, it may become a spiritual crisis in which one's personal life doesn't make sense anymore. It has become the frustrated, forgotten expression that has turned cancerous, eating away at our existence. It eats away at us, begging for our attention and our pledge to become its advocate. It wants its original forum for expression back, but we have forgotten what that was. We are only aware of the ailments and crisis we are now experiencing in its place. It tries to teach us that, in order to feel a sense of well-being within our life, we need to be true and honest with our internal expressions and desires.

These expressions and desires are those that belong to the soul and to this incarnation. They are the urges that the heart senses and feels compelled to follow along this path of authenticity. These expressions emanate from the soul, but are of the many nuances and parts comprising the incarnated, individual personality. In our incarnations here, upon this Earth school, we are learning expression of our soul in its full glory. The soul chooses to be incarnated on this plane in order to experience itself in a physical form conducive to interacting, learning, growing, and evolving. The soul's goal is to live the authentic life within this physical, human form. Creativity is the energy behind authenticity, propelling it into manifestation.

When we come to recognize our soul's expression as the splendor of the soul coming through and into our physical awareness, we begin to take ourself and our desires more seriously than before. This is what is required to live authentically. It requires us to be serious about our inner desires, our inner calling. We must not just view these ideas as fleeting thoughts, a "stage" to grow out of, or inconceivable dreams, but as the true inner expression of ourself, deserving our respect, trust, and honor. The more we trust and honor this part of ourself, the more we allow our creativity to develop and grow. The more we are honest and true to our own calling, the greater we will realize our personal creativity.

HOW DO I LIVE AUTHENTICALLY IN MY EVERYDAY LIFE?

Everyday authenticity can be a challenge. In our life there are mortgages to pay, mouths to feed, houses to clean, and jobs to work. There are deadlines, rules and regulations, and demands. There are numerous responsibilities that require our attention, time, and energy. So, where do we fit our authentic Self into the picture? The best suggestion would probably be, anywhere we can!

In actuality, if you don't make and take the time and space for yourself to incorporate your heartfelt desires and expressions into your life, you will most likely be met with cynicism, burn-out, or martyrdom down the road. No matter how busy or how chaotic your current life appears to be, promise yourself that you will invest time into your own dreams. Following, are practical suggestions for living authentically regardless of your demanding responsibilities.

Be present - Try to remain focused on the task or situation at hand. Avoid jumping   ahead of yourself and becoming overwhelmed. Bring yourself back to the present.

Be 100% - Give your all when you are engaging within a situation. If the situation is particularly demanding and tough, try to view it as a rewarding challenge. Give it your best shot by exerting your best efforts. Whenever possible, if you are not content with the situation, make what changes you can to be more fully engaged.

Be honest - Listen to your dreams and desires. Learn to say yes to yourself. Be able to say no when the situation commands.

Be able - Take the necessary time and space for yourself within your demanding schedule. Let yourself pursue your own interests. Maybe enroll in that class you have always wanted to take or begin the meditation routine at home that you have always intended. You'll never know what will become of it until you try.

Be open - Listen to your inner voice. Learn to trust this part of yourself. Really hear and act upon your inner calling. It knows your true purpose.

By including these elements within our life, we are helping ourself to live life to its fullest regardless of our current predicament, lifestyle, or challenge. By doing so, we are allowing ourself to grow into the authentic and significant being our soul knows we truly are.

We live in a Uni-verse with *uni* meaning *one* and *verse* meaning *a metrically arranged sequence*. In other words, our part in this Oneness stems from being an integral piece of this harmonious, patterned arrangement. We are all a specific part of the verse, a piece of the full sonnet. To belittle or ignore our part in this unified work, in fact, is a disservice to the Uni-verse. Each part is important to the others as each helps create the composite arrangement. So what each of us can fully add to this cosmic symphony, this harmony of life, is of utmost importance to the creation of this perfectly balanced ballad of authenticity. The ballad of your life.

Chapter 7 - CREATIVE COMMUNION

The time has come for us to own our voice. This means communicating who we truly are. Expressing our soul's calling is paramount. When we are on the path of learning to accept and own the power of creativity, we actualize this energy outwardly through expressing ourself within the world. Once we have established the inner connection with our own unique essence of creativity, this link can propel us forward and on purpose.

This link is a powerful connection to our world. How we communicate ourself outwardly says a lot about our soul's intent. If we withhold our true expression, for whatever reason, then we are withholding the true expression of our soul. When we limit our true expression, then we are limiting the true intent of our soul.

In order to allow ourself to experience our soul's calling, we must learn to give our soul a voice on the physical plane. This means getting to know ourself, trusting what is inside, establishing a pure connection, and embracing the desire to bring forth an honest expression of ourself. When we do this, we begin to find events and circumstances within our life flowing with greater ease. It's not that they actually are; it's just that now we don's fight the current of life as much. Things still happen, but we feel increasingly more in synch with the happenings and trust a broader understanding of a purpose behind the "madness." We begin to see the connection between events in our life and our own special interplay with them. This brings us to a greater awareness of life with all of its interconnections. We are in communion with life and we have a voice, a channel, to express our part.

As we explore the various ways we suppress and/or expand our creative communion, our soul's voice, an image of a DOOR may be helpful to help illustrate this concept. A door can be opened and closed. It keeps things in and it keeps things out. Some doors can be locked when needed and require a key to be opened. Other doors are never locked, allowing access at all times. When we enter or exit through a door, we move across a threshold into another space. The door becomes the threshold guardian. Imagine your soul having a door. No one but yourself is in charge of this door. You hold the key and you control the lock. Energy in the form of creative expression resides behind this door. The energy of your spirit and the intent of your soul exists there waiting to be expressed. It is your decision whether or not you wish to invite this expression into your life. All it takes is the opening of a door.

SOUL INTENT
What does your soul intend for you? Is it ever possible to know this? Our souls are constantly speaking to us. They tell us who were are, but first, we must learn how to listen before we can know our soul's

intent. When we begin to understand our soul's intent, we can follow, honor, and live our purpose, and thus, move into a space of creative empowerment.

The language of the soul is not constructed from rules of sentence structure and proper grammar. This is not to say that the soul is uneducated or illiterate, but the soul has its own form of communication. Its style of communication is more poetic than prosaic. The soul is of the imaginal world, comprised of images, thoughts, feelings, and intuitive forces. It speaks to us from the atmosphere in which it dwells. It speaks to us in flashes of insight. It communicates through dreams. It offers intuitive thoughts and reveries of images. Many of us miss our soul's messages because we dismiss these poetic activities as foolishly silly, impractical, imaginary, and unimportant. By doing so, we disregard the message. We shut out our soul.

It takes practice and time to trust and honor this type of communication that is welling up inside of us. We must learn to welcome these muses. This language of the soul can inspire us to live the type of life we came here to live. It can help us remember our true spiritual nature. It reminds us of who we are. The soul is of the imaginal and of the spiritual. The soul transcends ethnicity, color, creed, and personality. It takes us right to the core of who we are. It rejoices with creative energy pulsating throughout our physical, human form when we acknowledge its existence within our awareness. We bring awareness of it into our life when we offer respect to our soul's presence.

HOW DO I INCREASE AN AWARENESS OF MY SOUL?

There are many ways to live a more soulful life and become increasingly aware of our soul. What's important is that we are not just acknowledging our soul's existence, but that we are allowing its existence to enter into our life. This means being ready, willing, and able to honor our intuitions and insights. It means welcoming our dreams and remaining open to our inner truths. It means readily embracing who we really are at our core, yet also accepting all of the roles we have played and the hats we have worn which make us who we are today, regardless of whether or not we like the present outcome.

The following is a list of ways to practice being in communion with your soul. They can serve as guideposts to help you increase this awareness and invite soul into your life.

Dreams - Recording your dreams and reading over them can help shed light on your current situations. The symbols are powerful and contain personal meaning specific to the dreamer. Work with your symbols by exploring your associations to them. Apply these associations to your dream. Let your dreams live by creating artwork that is inspired by dream content. Listen to the artwork. (Read more about working with dreams later in this chapter.)

Intuition - The next time you experience an intuitive hunch, write it down. If you decide not to listen to it, at least acknowledge it. Recording it sends a signal to your soul that you are receiving the information. This, in turn, confirms that the message as being honored. As a result, more intuitive insights will come.

Images - Many people receive flashes of pictures in their minds that linger with them. These images need to be honored as a form of inner communication. Record these representations through drawings, writing, and poetry. These images have something to say, maybe psychic, intuitive, or prophetic.

Most importantly, learn to listen to yourself. This requires a listening that is not always done with the ear. This type of hearing may come via feelings, sensations, and thoughts in addition to the aforementioned ways.

We need to explore the ways we suppress our creative communion. When we lose sight of our dreams and our personal truths, we suppress our ability to live a creatively fulfilling life. There are different reasons for why we lose this sight. However, in many cases, we have simply blocked our sight, blocked our dreams and truths.

SOUL REPRESSION

Today, in Western society, depression has become mainstream. Feeling depressed has become all too common. It is a serious illness affecting many, many people. People who experience the wrath of depression feel low in spirits, low in energy, apathetic, a decrease in their life force, a decrease in their activity, and many times feel immobile to do anything. To be "depressed," in literal terms, means to be flattened as with a downward pressure being exerted from above. In other words, being "pushed down" is what it means to be depressed. Therefore, depressed people feel a heaviness bearing down upon them as if things and circumstances within their life are weighing them down. They feel they have no control and can only narrowly identify their existence with the depression. The heaviness causes lethargy, inactivity, and immobility.

I once had a conversation with a woman in which she was discussing her experience with depression. At the time of our conversation, she was feeling better, but when she felt fully immersed within the midst of depression, she felt as if her whole existence was depressed. She believed if her whole existence felt depressed, how could her soul have remained untouched by this unwelcomed guest, depression?

I have my own angle on depression. I explained to her that I believe her soul was never depressed and it was, in fact, untouched. However, I did not deny the depression of her ego. I further explained that she had realized, through the various ways she worked through her depression, there was more to her existence than the depressed identity the depression convinced her of and gave her. Earlier in her depression, her ego chose to identify with the depression as that is what the ego knows to do when in the throes of heavy feelings. The ego reacts and responds. It's a matter of cause and effect. A heaviness was weighing upon her and her ego felt the effects and as a result, felt depressed. Depression is about a human, ego experience; who she is at the core is not at all identified with the depression. It is separate from the experience of depression. The soul is never limited in its experience. She stopped identifying with the depression as she began exploring the many facets of herself. She found a way through the depression as she came to know herself better; who she is, what is important to her, what her dreams/goals are, what her inner voice is saying. She began to pay attention. She began to attend to her soul. She came to know who she is again at her core existence and she allowed it to have voice.

This is not about underestimating the power that depression can have over us for it is a real issue with real concerns. This is only to say that when we feel this downward pressure, this heaviness, our tendency is to become all too consumed by it and therefore, to expand this heaviness into all areas of our life. This results in immobility. We change from being a "person with symptoms of depression" to a "depressed person," existing secondarily to the depression.

I believe that the soul is never depressed, in fact, it's untouched in very much the same way it is untouched by death. The energy continues on. However, the ego is very powerful indeed. As a soul steps aside much like a master would do for his/her student and allows the ego, the personality, to learn its lessons regardless of the pain and regardless of the results, the ego comes to feel empowered. The ego takes on the world, including the world of depression, and becomes consumed by the experience, thus, obtaining its identity from it.

An interrelationship between "ego depression" and "soul repression" exists. A repression of the soul is the main cause of this illness. To be repressed means to be kept down, held back, or restrained. When we are in the midst of a repression, we are being prevented and kept from a natural development and expression of whatever is being repressed. Feeling depressed and being repressed are two different, yet related, things. As was described earlier, being depressed is about feeling flattened with a sense of exerted downward pressure and a decrease in activity. Repressed is about being held back and restrained where a natural expression and development is prevented. The soul never experiences depression, but it does experience repression. This repression is the foundation for the human experience of depression. When the soul's intent is repressed and not permitted to express, develop, expand, and be itself, the ego comes to feel restrained. When the ego, the personality, is affected by this restraint, this repression and depression will eventually result. The ego has taken on the guilt, the shame, or the fear that stems from repressing important aspects of ourself.

Picture the ego as a vehicle that is fueled by gasoline energy.

Picture the soul as the gasoline (the energy). When it is necessary for the vehicle to travel, gas is needed. In a sense, the vehicle is alive when it is moving and running off of its fuel. When the fuel is withheld or not replenished, the vehicle is stuck and immobile. In a similar manner the ego (our human vehicle) experiences immobility caused by the withdrawal and repression of the soul's intent (its energy). This is a very real experience that causes numbness and lack of energy.

Depression is the result of the soul being detrimentally affected; its energy has been withheld. The soul, on some level, has been thwarted in development and in the expression of itself. In other words, depression stems from our soul, our core existence, being held back, repressed, and not being allowed to express or be who or what we really are. We feel depressed when enough of our soul experience is not allowed to feel love and/or be loved. We feel depressed when we don't live our truths. We feel depressed when we don't express who we are, what we are about, or our gifts. We feel depressed when <u>we blame ourself</u> and carry the weight of our shame and guilt. The outward experience of depression is not about what the exhibiting depressed feelings appear to be. The depressed feelings are actually about the restraint the soul experiences as it is being kept from its true expressions. When we relearn to be true to ourself, the depression lifts, the repressed era ends, and our soul learns to breathe again.

Depression is about a journey with a lesson in mind. It teaches us to go down into the underworld with the filth, mire, and muck, with the pressing of the earth's crust weighing heavy upon our back. This heavy crust is comprised from all of the leftovers and debris, when combined, becomes nutrients. These nutrients are the key ingredients we have left behind, alone, and ignored within ourself. A return to mother earth teaches us that the scraps of compost have become sweet-smelling soil embracing us within its nutrients, nurturing our growth and attempting to bring us back to our underlying truths. The depression takes us into the pits, pushing us to dig up and cultivate our repressed dreams.

We grow when we come to understand our soul's desire to bloom, to express these hidden and forgotten pieces. When we come to understand that compost provides the much needed, helpful nutrients despite its origin of debris, we begin to bloom. Our soul blossoms when we believe in and support the expression of our heart's desire. The heart's desire, this creative passion, is our true calling. It is the calling of our soul. This is about being who we are, foregoing the collective "shoulds," and permitting the true expression of ourself. This is not so easy to do, in fact, it is tough, but as we remind ourself to listen to our own hearts rather than to the "shoulds" of others, we begin to move closer to our empowerment. Expression of our calling removes the hands of repression and the weight of depression. We can then reemerge singing our own song and dancing the dance of our soul, our own individualized and specialized triumphant dance. This is a life-long dance that continually requires new steps, but only we can dance our own steps.

HOW DO I HELP MY EGO STEP THROUGH THE DEPRESSION?

One of the most important things you can do for yourself is to try not to turn off or shut down your depressed ego. When we do, this tends to make matters worse and complicate the situation even more so. We can't ignore a part of ourself just like we can't ignore the proverbial elephant sitting in our living room. Depression is not something we can turn our back on, as it is a painful, open doorway to our soul. A good therapist or qualified practitioner is recommended to assist you in your journey inwards.

Consider keeping a journal (written and drawn) and incorporating visualizations into your daily routine. These will serve as your companions during your trek through depression. Establish a structure for your expressions such as a time and place to write, draw, and visualize your current emotions. This commitment will help you get more in touch with these emotions, including the apathetic ones. As Carl Gustav Jung said, "Emotion is the chief source of all becoming consciousness. There can be no transforming of darkness into light or of apathy into movement without emotion." Your emotions will serve as the vessel (the energy in motion) taking you to the underlying message of your depression. From there you can discover what you have been repressing.

I am encouraging you to take an active stance with your depression. When people are feeling depressed, they generally do not want to do anything. Desire dies and movement ceases. By making an agreement with yourself to record your experience and to use visualizations, you are making a major step in the direction of lifting the depression and ending the repressed era. You might also find other alternative activities you can use in place of visualizations. These include, but are not limited to, body work, breath work, meditation, and group work. Do, however, keep a visual journal in addition to exercising these other modalities.

Following, is a journal exercise that combines the processes of visualizing, drawing, and writing. Many clients and workshop participants have found this specific exercise helpful and successful for uncovering and releasing painful emotions. It is broken down into three steps. As with any exercise suggested in this book, trust your own process.

Directions -

X-ray Visualization

Part 1: **Visualizing**

Sit at a table with your journal and colors (markers, crayons, or other media) in front of you. Close your eyes and slowly breathe in and out. Take a few moments and just breathe. As you breathe, focus your

129

awareness on your body. (Pause.) Now, with your mind's eye, allow it to scan your being. Notice any type of sensation you may feel. Scan your major organs and each part of your body. The sensation may be experienced as a stiffness, a tightness, a numbness, an emotion, or any other feeling you may notice. You may feel and/or visually see in your mind's eye the sensation. Notice how it feels. Pay attention to how it moves. Imagine how it looks. (Pause.) Make a mental picture of it and move on to the next sensation. Focus on each one you discover. (Pause.) When you feel you have finished scanning your whole being, bring all that you have experienced back with you as you open your eyes.

Part 2: **Drawing**

Open your journal to a fresh sheet of paper•· Choose a color and draw a representative outline of your body on the paper. Try to fill the page with this outline as this will give you enough room in which to work. When finished, you will have an inside and an outside to the body-form on the paper (like a cookie-cutter shape). Now, recall the sensations and feelings you noticed as you scanned your being. With each sensation, choose the color(s) that best represents it. Draw the sensation in its corresponding place on the body-form on your paper.

• Before you start, remember that any art exercise described in this book has been suggested to you for your own benefit and not for aesthetic purposes. With this in mind, remind yourself that your drawing ability does not factor into this exercise nor any other.

Show its feelings, movements, and looks. Proceed with these instructions for each sensation you discovered. Just do your best to capture the sensations.

Part 3: **Writing**

When you are finished drawing, you are now ready for the writing part. Look at your x-ray drawing. It depicts what you are currently experiencing. Each drawn sensation has something to say. Focus on one sensation at a time and let it speak. Use a writing utensil and write next to the image exactly what each specific sensation has to say. This can be written outside of the body-form or on another page of the journal. Really listen to the messages. Take your time and record the feelings.

Once you have recorded all that the images want to say, you can now use another sheet of paper in your journal and dialogue with the sensations. Imagine how the conversations would go if you and your feelings could speak to each other. Well, I know that you actually can speak with your feelings! I have witnessed it happen too many times to believe otherwise. Trust what you hear and feel. Explore with each sensation its purpose, its feelings, and its message.

This series of exercises should be repeated often to continue your dialogue with any withstanding emotions and sensations. Use these exercises as you journey inward to explore an existing depression.

Remember, the depression holds you down and takes you within to force you to shift and make changes. Constructively channeling the depressed feelings in this manner provides your creative essence the permission to flow and to help you grow. These exercises help you communicate with the related feelings and can bring you an understanding of what has been repressed.

SLEEP-WALKING THROUGH LIFE

When a body sleep-walks, the body goes through the motions without the waking mind being conscious of what it's doing. It is as if the body is on automatic pilot while the mind is aware of only the dream. Many of us approach life on automatic pilot. We sleep-walk through life. We go through the motions, do what we're told, do what we should do, do what we're supposed to do, and do, do, do all over ourself while we remain unconscious to this trance.

We know we are sleep-walking through life when all of a sudden, one day, we wake up and begin to ask ourself, "What is the meaning of all of this?" We have been playing by the rules, we've been passing GO and collecting our 200 dollars, but all the while we have been going in circles, around and around. We feel purposeless and apathetic. We are tired of playing the game! When we stop and ask ourself, "What is the meaning of all of this?" we truly begin to wake up. This is the point at which we begin to wipe the sleep out of our eyes and allow our sight to regain focus after a deep sleep.

We soon understand that there is not a game manual, a prescribed way, we are supposed to live our life. There is not a certain amount of status we are supposed to reach or a certain amount of money we need to have in the bank or a specific level we must attain in order to be successful. Instead, we learn there is a large part of ourself that has been unexpressed, that has been asleep. Sometimes it takes an incredible event within our life that shocks us out of our deep sleep. At other times, the wake-up call can come about by the individual's search for meaning. We wake up when we come to the crossroads in life that require us to ask deep, philosophical questions about our existence and about our purpose. Sometimes the wake-up call comes traumatically as in the case of individuals who have experienced close calls with death, for example, near death experiences (N.D.E.s), or have experienced the loss of a loved one, or maybe the loss of a job. When the wake-up call comes, we can be taken by surprise, caught off guard, which is usually the case, and sent into the spinning desire to make sense of the event. At other times, we may become so shocked and overwhelmed by the event that we become disgruntled with the whole event itself. When this happens, we sometimes miss our current wake-up call and the inherent lesson of the event. We hit the snooze button instead.

When I was young, I used to sleep-walk. I would end up all over the house. I remember one time being awakened in the kitchen where I was trying to find the bathroom. Another time, I got up, got dressed, made my bed, and was ready to go to school. All of this occurring at three o'clock in the morning! My mother came in and woke me up. I realized I was just a bit early for class that morning. I was surprised, shocked, amazed, and embarrassed with all I could accomplish in this state while never being conscious. I wondered, "how could I have been asleep through all of this?"

I believe that when we do awaken from the deep sleep and trance our life has been under, we too are shocked, amazed, and may even want to kick ourself for being asleep for so long. But while we are in the sleep, we are not even aware that we are under this trance. It is all too easy to go through life and not know that we are merely sleep-walking through it.

HOW DO I KNOW IF I HAVE BEEN SLEEP-WALKING THROUGH LIFE?

Here is a constructed list of several scenarios to ask yourself about that can help you determine whether or not you have been sleep-walking through life:

Being busy keeping up with the Joneses

Are you concerned with outer approval and appearance?

Do you buy, lease, purchase, secure loans just to have what everybody else has?

Do your material things make you feel important?

This is about being concerned with our status and appearances. We tend to find our self-worth in who we know and what we own. It becomes an endless cycle perpetuated by our imprisonment to the things we own and the things we think we need. This is a syndrome in which we must have more, we must have better, faster, and newer.

Chasing the Golden Carrot

Are you so focused on the end result that you forget the process of living life?

Are you spending excessive time away from your loved ones because you are chasing the almighty dollar?

This is a scenario in which we go after one thing only to discover when we obtain it there is really more to have. We feel unsettled because there is always more. This is an incessant cycle. We continue on and on, trying to find contentment in what we pursue by being eluded by the happiness we just know it promises us. This is about never being happy and content with the present.

Subscribing to peer pressure

Do you feel a need to fit in?

Do you try to be normal?

Do you do something and want something because they do?

Are you easily influenced by the words and actions of others?

This is when we are concerned about being like everybody else.

Typically, we don't want attention drawn to ourself for being different, except for when the attention proves that we are the same as everyone else. We feel if we are different we won't be approved of or liked. This is when we definitely seek that seal of approval from others.

Following prescribed roles

Do you do the line of work you do because you were outwardly encouraged to do so?

Did you get married, start a family, buy a house because others were doing so?

Do you behave a certain way because that's what a woman does, that's what a man does?

This is about following and adhering to the collective roles that were expected of us. These expected roles could have been instilled by family, school, church, place of employment, or by your culture. Following the prescribed roles keeps us being just one of the flock. When we do so, we do so at the expense of losing our individuality and our own identity.

Remaining within unpleasant situations

Do you just remain at your place of employment even though you have been experiencing burnout because its comfortable or because you want to make it to retirement?

Do you stay in a relationship with a friend, spouse, or mate when you are degraded and/or abused?

This is about becoming complacent, resigned, or apathetic. Low self-esteem and low self-worth are its biggest allies. When we don't feel good about ourself we tend to think that there is not any better circumstance or situation out there for us, and therefore, we develop the I'd better just accept my lot in life attitude.

Disregarding your dreams

Did you bury, give up, or replace your dreams for the wants of others?

Do you consider your dreams fleeting fantasies that are not rooted in reality?

Do you believe your dreams will get you no where and you are better off if they stay in your mind?

Do you disregard your heart's desire and your soul's calling?

This is about shutting yourself off from your true purpose and inner calling. This is about negating the faith in yourself and in your ability to pursue your desire. We can shut this off, lock it away, place it on the back burner, but we can never fully escape it. We may consciously forget about our dreams, but they will linger on crying for our attention. We may even project our own disbelief in our dreams onto those of others by commenting on how foolish "so-and-so" has become for going after his/hers.

Do any of these situations describe you? If so, you may have been sleep-walking through life. When we begin to explore and examine the beliefs we hold about ourself and our life, we begin to answer our wake-up call. We begin to realize there is more to ourself and to our existence than what we have been previously aware of in the past. We learn that we are more than just a physical being born, growing up, working hard, and then dying. We come to realize there is a lot more to life than originally assumed. When we wake up, we see that we are incredible beings with a true purpose and calling within this Universe. We stretch, yawn, and turn off that snooze button permanently. There is a purpose within us and we need to let it prevail!

Now, let's explore the ways we can expand our creative communion, our soul's voice. Our soul has a voice striving for expression. The dream realm provides such a forum for expression. When we work with our dreams, we honor this forum and invite soul into our life. Living a soulful life stirs passion. Passion awakens us and provides us a sense of purpose for following our dreams.

THE DREAM REALM

The dream realm is very important to the existence of the soul. It is within the dream realm where the soul can maintain its integrity. In a dream we can experience anything. Anything goes. We can fly through the skies, we can breathe under water, we can move from scene to scene, we can communicate with animals, and we can be any age, any sex, and any form. In a dream, we can experience intruders who chase us, only to discover they mean us no harm and really are our allies in disguise, once we learn to face them. We can do anything in the dream realm.

The dream realm is limitless. The expression of our soul is limitless also. It is infinite. Physics teaches us that energy is neither created nor destroyed, it just changes form. The energy of our total Self, which is of the soul, is neither created nor destroyed, but perseveres by changing form. Our soul, like energy studied in physics, follows the same principles. The soul is not a logical construct that is encased inside of this fleshy existence known as the human body. It goes beyond this existence; it is much bigger than this. It is a source of energy and light that extends beyond the human body and transcends the human experience. It is within and without the human form.

The soul knows no limitations. We, in a physical, human experience, learn to accept and create limitations for ourself. The soul does not interfere with the development of the personality and the arrangement of our personal limitations. We are here on earth, this classroom of lessons, for developing our soul. Our soul develops through lessons of the personality, the ego. A personality is developed within each incarnation for the purpose of learning. The soul is the energy source that remembers all and knows all, including its distant incarnations. It is that place in us and outside of us that fully understands the laws of creation. Being in this fleshy existence known as the human body, we forget our experience of the soul and we solely learn to rely upon and believe in the so-called physical experiences we hear, see, taste, touch, and smell around us. We tend to rely upon our five senses. The soul goes beyond the experience of the five senses. The soul allows us, as Gary Zukov, best-selling author, scientist, and philosopher, explains in the book, <u>Seat of the Soul,</u> to experience ourselves as "multidimensional" beings. A multidimensional being is one who goes beyond the five senses and develops a trust in intuitive insights and awarenesses. A sixth sense is cultivated. This individual comes to honor that part of him/herself that transcends the human, physical form. However, we have to work at it. We tend to forget that intuitive and psychic insights are a part of both our physical existence and spiritual inheritance.

When we dream, we tap into this limitless inheritance once again. We go into a realm in which anything goes and anything can happen. In Jungian dream analysis[*], we learn that all of the characters in the dream represent an aspect of ourself. We are the producers of our stage show for the evening as we are also the actors, the props, and the sets presenting this nocturnal theater that unfolds during our sleep.

In order for the soul to maintain its integrity and to help remind the personality of its limitless and infinite inheritance, it requires help.

---

[*]   A form of dream interpretation based upon the work of the late psychiatrist Carl G. Jung. He postulated a theory of universal matrix of consciousness to which all forms of life are connected. We relate to each other because of this collective influence. In Jungian Psychology, symbolism is both archetypal and personal. Dreams are explored to understand these symbolic connections.

While the soul exists in the physical with our body and personality, it simultaneously exists in the incorporeal where we can learn to encounter it in altered states of awareness such as in meditations, hypnosis, relaxation, focused awareness, and the dream realm. Since the soul is more expansive than the corporeal encasement within which we find ourself during this physical incarnation as a human being, it maintains aspects of itself, "fragments," within both the dream realm and the physical experience. The soul helps the personality remember its limitless existence by maintaining its hold within a limitless environment, such as the dream realm while simultaneously existing within the limiting human existence. That is why when we dream we have limitless abilities within our dreams. The personality, through dreams, has the opportunity to experience infinite possibilities. In dreams we are actually meeting up with our soul, that part of our soul that maintains its integrity by remaining within this dream realm of limitless thoughts, intentions, and existences. When we dream we experience these aspects of ourself that Jungian Psychology understands. In this case the dream represents parts of ourself, parts of our soul, and parts of our existence.

The soul also has a clear knowing of all that has happened to it, of all that it has experienced throughout eternity. That is why in dreams, as well as during other forms of altered awareness, we can experience past incarnations. Our dreams will show them to us as they pertain to our personal evolution. What is experienced is all relevant to the individual's soul. Some of the issues that we are working on, as past life therapy teaches us, come from past incarnations. Some of the issues we encounter in dreams may actually be issues we have been working on for generations, for eras, perhaps eons. To the soul there is no sense of linear time. Everything is occurring simultaneously at this present moment. The information we receive in dreams is helpful regardless of whether we know it is from a past life or the present incarnation. It is all information we can use just to understand our journey that much more.

As we explore our dreams, we can come to understand more about ourself. We can learn more about our bigger existence as the soul. We can also learn about our existence as the personality, the ego, in the present physical incarnation. Dreams can be very informative and helpful if we are willing to look at them and listen to them. There is no need to interpret dreams, but there is a need to explore them. Dreams can very well give us information to be understood on many different levels. A sole interpretation would abort the process of allowing all the different possibilities to be born out of the dream. For example, we may come to understand one way of viewing the dream one day and a new and different way the next. Because of this, dreams can be helpful if we just listen to the dream. This process allows us to nurture the dream to evolve and grow with us as we evolve and grow.

To explore a dream means to be fully open to the dream's

unfolding. The dream unfolds while we are experiencing the dream in the moment and while we are recalling our dreams in the waking state. An interpretation of a dream kills this process of unfolding. When we think we know what a dream means, we stop the dream dead in its tracks. This stops the ability to explore the multiple levels of a dream. Each dream can be viewed on many different levels. It's important to look at all these different levels as these different levels will help us fully to explore the dream from many different angles. For example, a dream can be seen as being literal, as being symbolic, and/or as being prophetic. When we choose one way of viewing the dream over another way, we do so at the expense of losing the other possible messages and insights contained within the dream. Many of us remember our dreams and find ourself recalling bits and pieces of them throughout the day. We may even share our dream with a close friend or spouse. We may even write down our dreams and review them at a later date. Paying tribute to the dream in this manner helps keep the dream alive. It helps keep the energy that is coming to us in symbols, in signs, and in images flowing. The more we are open to this energy, the more we provide access for it to flow into our life and consequently, the more we allow soul to be present within our daily life. The dream supports great insight and awareness of our soul. The soul speaks to us through these sleep-time visitors. The more we work with our dreams, the more conscious we become of this part of ourself which shows itself within dreams.

Writing down our dreams gives us the opportunity to explore our dreams within the waking state, bringing soul to light.

Dreams present their content in symbolic ways that are specific to the individual and to his/her relationship with others. This means that each person alone holds all the keys for unlocking and understanding his/her own dreams. In other words, we do not need dream dictionaries to tell us what this and that means. We only need our own associations and insights while we relate and review our dreams. Exploring dreams is like decoding a secret message. The soul provides us with dreams, these secret messages, to help us understand and make sense of our experiences as a human being. As we explore our dreams, we learn to work with and work through specific issues. We also learn to acknowledge, honor, and own specific strengths and abilities. Overall, exploring dreams helps us become more in touch with all aspects of who we truly are.

Dreams have a very important purpose within our life as they do allow us to come back in contact with our limitless inheritance. They allow us to be more fully in touch with our soul, that part of ourself that really knows who we are. Incredible insight and awareness can be gained at the level of our physical experience as we work with our dreams. The soul, this energy, this light, this unique expression of who we truly are, understands its predicament. It chooses to reside partly in the dream realm and partly in the physical realm in order to keep us connected to the spirit of creativity, our ability to grow and evolve spiritually. This situation is perfect just the way it is. Our soul is helping our personality evolve, learn, and grow in each incarnation our soul inhabits. In turn, this expansion helps the soul evolve and grow, to understand more fully its connection to the source of all creation.

The dream realm provides a forum to experiment with and experience limitless thought. The more we work with dreams in the waking realm, the more we become open to working with dreams while we are dreaming. This state is known to many as becoming lucid. The state of lucid dreaming allows the dreamer to have conscious awareness that he/she is dreaming while in the dream state. This conscious awareness can help the dreamer explore his/her limitless abilities while in the limitless realm of dreams. When we become lucid, we can fly, we can travel to different places, we can communicate within anyone we choose, we can confront attackers, and we can do all sorts of interesting phenomena at will. This forum becomes the place where we reconnect with the aspects of our soul that reside within the dream realm. We reconnect with those parts of ourself that bring a more conscious awareness to us in our waking life, a more conscious awareness of who we really are.

Whether we explore our dreams from recorded material or while we are actually within the dream, we are bringing ourself more in touch with all aspects of ourself. We are allowing ourself to be in communion with our soul. When we are in touch with who we truly are, in touch with our soul, we begin to feel more empowered within our life. We begin to understand more about our specific purpose within our human experience. Most importantly, we tap into the divine, creative power that resides within each of us. Exploring our dreams helps us become more empowered and more in touch with the essence of ourself. This allows us to access truth and come to know our soul's calling. Exploring brings us deeper into this awareness. Exploring helps bring a soulful life to the personality.

HOW DO I EXPLORE THE MULTI-MEANINGS OF DREAMS?

Learning to explore the multi-meanings of dreams is a skill that takes time to cultivate. Not only does it take time and patience, but it requires a keen ability to listen. The dreamer must learn to explore the dream from different angles, be open to many possibilities, and hear the manifold messages.

The first step for working with your dreams is to form a habit of writing down your dreams upon awakening. Never wait until after you shower, have your morning coffee, or go to work because the dream will begin to dissipate over time. Catch it while it's fresh. Record all details no matter how trivial something may appear to be. Don't fill in any gaps. Dreams are not meant to follow a logical frame of thought. Just record them as they are. If you believe that you are one of those people who doesn't dream, nonsense, everybody dreams! In fact, if you receive seven or eight hours of sleep per night, you will have approximately five dreams. To begin remembering your dreams, tell yourself before you go to sleep at night that you will remember your dreams. Leave your journal by your bedside, open and ready for recording. Lastly, but most importantly, you must <u>want</u> to recall your dreams. Once this is in place, you are ready to enter the realm of dream content. Following, are suggestions for getting you started on exploring, hearing, and learning from your dreams.

Story - Record the dream. Notice the overall plot of the dream. What story like this is unfolding in my life?

Environment - Review the setting of the dream. What does this place remind me of emotionally, physically, mentally, and spiritually?

Atmosphere - Remember the feelings of the dream. What did I feel in the dream or when I awoke? What is familiar about this feeling? What in my life feels like this?

Characters - Explore what the characters are like. What part of myself is like that dream character? What behavior of my own is likened to the dream character?

Symbols - Notice the major symbols and explore <u>your</u> associations to them. What are my own understandings and ideas about the symbols? What do they mean to me, my culture, my environment, and my society? Do the dream associations relate to my life?

Message - Listen to the message(s). Hear it literally, metaphorically, and symbolically. How many different ways can I hear this message?

Word-play - Observe multi-meanings. Look for puns, cliches, metaphors, and colloquialisms. For example, if you dream about having a big nose, ask yourself: Am I a <u>nosy</u> person? Do I stick my <u>nose</u> where it is unwanted? Do I tell lies and my <u>nose</u> grows (like Pinnochio)? Maybe I <u>nose</u> (know) too much?

After exploring the dream via the aforementioned ways, set the dream aside. Come back to it at a later time and notice how more insights may come to you regarding the dream. By not ascribing one interpretation to the dream, you allow the image of the dream to live on inside of you in limitless possibilities. It continues to provide you with rich information about yourself and your soul. A dream which stays alive helps keep creativity awake.

AWAKEN WITH PURPOSE

Everyone has a purpose. Life's events tend to flow smoothly and our responses and reactions to them flow more readily when we are "on purpose." Instead of just finding ourself reacting to life, we find ourself initiating life as a co-creator instrumental in the movement of our life.

Knowing our purpose is about knowing what our soul's calling is. When we know what this purpose is, then the next step is to allow the purpose to unfold within our life. We become proactive and allowing. As we do so, we find ourself receiving glimpses of the "bigger picture" of our life. We come to understand how the specific part we play in life relates to our life and to the lives of others. In this way we begin to see how everybody's life is orchestrated perfectly so the pieces fit together, comprising a beautiful opus.

When our purpose is clear to us, we don't have time for negativity. Instead of overindulging in substances, instead of carrying on with destructive habits, compulsive obsessions, lethargy, apathy, and immobility we tend to find ourself active and involved. Being on purpose is about being involved with the process of life. The more involved we become in our life, with ourself and with others, the more we will find ourself moving toward our purpose. Being focused on what we want helps us stay on purpose. When we know what we want, all of the resources that can help us with our purpose, that can provide us with the fulfillment of our purpose, will begin to show up in our life. It is as if our purpose magnetically draws to us the specific circumstances, people, and events that are necessary for its fulfillment. Being focused is an instrumental part of staying on purpose and fulfilling our soul's calling. There are many ways we can remain focused. One of the most important ways to remain focused is through our actions and through our thoughts, which become the arteries supporting the life of our dreams.

HOW DO I BECOME FOCUSED?
There are different ways we can help ourself find, develop, and maintain a focus in life. Being focused in life means finding ourself

concentrating upon and attending to our purpose. All of us are purposeful beings; we just need to awaken to our purpose within. Focus is what keeps us on our path of doing so. Many methods can help us gain and develop our focus. Here are several different techniques you can use.

Affirmations/Visualizations

These are powerful tools that help you keep a clear picture of what it is you wish to magnetize toward yourself. Affirmations are sentences either written or spoken in the present tense describing what you want to embody. Their power resides in your ability to feel them. Visualizations, on the other hand, are mental images you envision to help you draw the aspired state to you by power of the conscious mind. They both work by changing your beliefs and creating an effect upon conscious and subconscious levels.

Examples of affirmations:

I welcome opportunities into my life that allow me to develop my intuition.

I am a clear channel for creative expression.

I am at one with the flow of my life.

(and whatever else you want to manifest into your life)

Example of visualizations: Let's say that you want to improve your public speaking skills. Visualize yourself speaking in front of people with confidence and ease. In your minds eye see yourself speaking with confidence and being well received.

Relaxation

Exercises, recreations, and disciplines that promote relaxation can help you maintain a focus within your life. Yoga, meditation, walking, gardening and various other activities promote a retreat from everyday cerebral functioning. Engaging in these activities offers us an opportunity to recharge our spirit. This is not just an indulgence. Relaxation is absolutely necessary for a balanced and focused lifestyle.

Focused Intent/Action

This is about taking an active stance toward achieving your dreams and goals. You can't always sit around waiting for the right moment to present itself at your door. It's important to exert energy and action in the direction you wish to go. This active posture shows the universe that you are serious about your focus and are willing to do your part. Being active creates a vortex of energy around yourself drawing to you more action for attracting your goals.

Beliefs

The beliefs you harbor about your focus provide the answer to whether or not you will ever find yourself living your dreams and goals. If you believe that it really isn't possible to express your soul's calling, then the attitude you will exude will be, most likely, one of self-sabotage. Likewise, if you believe in your focus and in yourself, then you will emanate an attitude of self-confidence, drawing to you positive and helpful energy and situations.

The most important concept to understand here is that only you can make your soul's calling a reality. You have the power and ability to become aware of your life's purpose, to focus on it with active intent, and to take the steps necessary to manifest it in the physical world. For your own sake, and for the benefit of all the souls around you, don't miss this chance of a lifetime!

Chapter 8 - INTUITIVE CREATION

Being creative is about establishing a union between our intuitive feelings and our intellectual ideas. It means being an active participant in the conjoining of ingredients for creativity. We come to realize that we are merely alchemists transforming ourself through the creative visions we keep. When we realize the impact we can have upon the quality of our life and upon the lives of others, we grow increasingly more aware of the intuitive wisdom stewing inside of ourself. We learn that we can act upon these intuitive hunches and insights for we know that they are natural and inherent parts of ourself.

Our intellect and intuition are magical ingredients for creativity. It is from within our intellect that wishes, desires, and dreams are born. The thought to create dwells there. The pure, potential creative energy is a constant and ever-ready energy. It is limitless. All it needs is a channel to reveal its emergence from our intellect. Our intuitive faculties serve as the opening for creative energy to pour into our life. The dream gives it life, but our insights give it sustenance. When we accept and trust our intuitive perceptiveness, we feed this creative energy, nurturing it to grow.

You might find it helpful to envision the image of an EYE while learning about intuitive creation within this chapter. This eye is an all-knowing, all-seeing eye. Not unlike the concept of the spiritual, third

eye, it is able to see into various realms and situations while

ascertaining profound meaning and truth. It represents your ability to

do the same. All of us have the ability to bring greater clarity and

insight into our life continually. We just need to learn how to do this.

The following is an exercise in visualization used to help people

move into this place of empowerment represented by the symbol of the

third eye. It is an exercise that can be used frequently as it is easy to

do with practice.

Directions -

Activate All-knowing/seeing Abilities
Close your eyes and relax. Allow yourself to get comfortable.

Focus on your breathing and take slow and deliberate breaths. As you

breathe, allow yourself to become quiet. Release your thoughts of the

day. (Pause.) Imagine a spot at the center of your forehead. Breathe

into this spot. As you breathe into this spot, notice that it gently opens

and expands. A bright and warm light radiates at this spot. The spot

continues to expand. Take your time. (Pause.) The light becomes

inviting. This spot expands to the size of a doorway. When you are

ready, you may enter into this space. (Pause.) You are surrounded by a

warm glow. This space is sacred. It is a space of profound knowledge.

It is an all-knowing and all-seeing sanctum. In this space, you may ask

your Higher Self to share wisdom and insight into any situation within your life. This is the space within you that knows. Ask and listen and observe. The answer may come in the form of an image. The answer may come as a voice. The answer may be intuitively felt. Trust how it presents itself. Take your time. (Pause.) When you are complete, thank the wisdom. Return through the doorway of the expanded spot. Allow this spot to return to normal. Focus once again on your breathing. Open your eyes when you are ready. Welcome back.

You may use this exercise to receive clarity, guidance, and awareness regarding any situation in your life. You do have the answers for yourself within. With practice, you will be able to access this space more readily and receive instant discernment on the heart of the matter under question.

TRUSTING

Developing a trust in ourself is essential. Without self-trust, it is extremely hard and next to impossible to develop intuition. Intuition is just another way the creative energy channels itself. Insights of intuition rely upon our level of willingness to acknowledge them. They are always occurring, nonetheless, but our ability to notice these insights and benefit from them depends upon our openness to them. We must learn to trust ourself in order to trust our intuitive insights and the expression of our creativity.

Creative energy thrives on self-trust. To be able to express ourself more fully in the world requires trust. To allow ourself to be truly faithful to our soul's path, we must feel a commitment of trust to our deeper purpose. This trust enables us to move forward on our unique path even when life seems to provide its distractions and obstacles. When we trust our deeper purpose, we learn to trust ourself and how we travel along this journey. Distractions and obstacles become tools and challenges when we trust the process of our unfolding purpose.

Sometimes it is really hard to trust ourself because, after all, we may have created circumstances in our life that have been downright ugly and painful. We tend to blame ourself for these circumstances. Yes, we are responsible for our own well-being. However, what we knew back then and what we know now makes all the difference. We might not have known the extent of the influence we could have exerted upon our life back then. We might not have realized we had free will and choice. What we did back then was just what we did; it was the best we could do at the time even if it was self-defeating. We must learn to accept ourself despite our mistakes and failures. We needlessly punish ourself for them. We don't realize that they can be our greatest teachers, but they can and they are! It is in the present where we can, now, forgive ourself. It is in the present where we can be honest with ourself. It is this self-honesty that can be trusted. It is time to ask ourself to be our own best friend. It is now time to trust this friend.

HOW DO I INCREASE SELF-TRUST?
Trust in ourself is a key that unlocks a very big door. Intuitive

abilities await behind this door. When we unlock this door with our key of trust, we invite this aspect of creativity into our life. We can learn to channel this intuitive creativity to glimpse the bigger picture of life. By honoring this part of ourself, we are increasing the opportunities to open to our true potentials. We are enabling our soul to share its wisdom within our human existence. We are allowing ourself to merge more and more with our soul's calling.

We learn to trust ourself when we take our intuition more seriously. As was suggested in the previous chapter, this means acknowledging our intuition. The expressions, the insights, the ideas, and the dreams that emerge from within us hold relevance. All of creation is born from within. Treat your own conceptions with respect.

Following are several suggestions to help increase the level of trust you have for yourself. Try them out and determine what works for you. You will probably have your own ideas to add to this list.

Honesty - Be honest with yourself about how you feel, what your goals are, and who you are.

Honor - Hold yourself sacred, honor the expressions of yourself whether they are verbal, written, or visual.

Listen - Hear what you have to say, really listen to yourself.

Communicate - Provide yourself the space to speak, acknowledge your opinion; this may be in the form of writing a journal or an actual dialogue with others.

Self-time - Generate time for yourself so you can be alone with your thoughts.

Share - Share of yourself, your ideas, dreams, desires, and goals with others who support you.

KNOWING

When we know something, we are clear about it. We may experience a "gut" feeling or an intuitive knowing about something or someone. This clear reaction or response signals to ourself that we "just know "even though we might not always be sure as to how we "just know." Knowing is about understanding, not necessarily understanding how things work, but understanding that things just are.

When we know that something is, we tend not to question it. This can be dangerous if we blindly accept the dogma of others as our own truths. Knowing is not about blind acceptance. It is about learning our own truths. We learn our own truths, those that are inherent to our own soul, when we have instilled a trust in ourself. By allowing ourself to develop this level of trust, we lay the foundation for the emanation of our truths.

Not everybody's truths will be synonymous. We are all on different levels of growth and spiritual evolution, thus, we all have different paths to travel. Therefore, we must determine our own way, the way that makes the most sense to our soul. There will always be those people who you really "click" with, for you will find that you have similar paths to follow and may hold similar truths. People will come and go during our lifetime, but that is because our paths must now go different ways, unique and specific to our own growth.

When we understand this concept of knowing, it becomes harder and harder to deny our soul's calling because we are getting to know ourself. In fact, it becomes easier and easier to express ourself. Though, many times we may find ourself within careers, lifestyles, relationships, and structures that don't seem to fit us anymore; we discover we just can't do it this way any longer. The way we have been doing things doesn't seem to make that much sense. We may be experiencing a deadening of our spirit. When this happens, we have come to a place in our life where we must start living our truths. We can't hide from them anymore. This comes with the territory of developing an awareness of ourself and of knowing ourself.

This does not mean we must leave our careers, change our lifestyles, end our relationships, or be done with any form of structure. Instead, we must find ways to include the true, creative expression of our soul's calling within our life. In some cases, it may mean making some drastic changes, especially if you have been feeling soulless in some area of your life. At this stage in the journey, you know that you hold the responsibility for the quality of life you desire to lead, and in most cases, you will be drawn to discovering ways of including your budding expression within your current life. You are like a flower that is growing and you need an environment that is supportive of your blooming. You will be drawn to create this for yourself.

As we come to trust our intuition, we come to know more about our creative essence. The intuition that guides us is the voice of our creative essence. When we listen, it teaches us to live life not only with our physical, five senses, but also enhanced by our developing ability (our psychic, sixth sense) to intuit, discern, and therefore, know.

SUPPORT THE DEVELOPMENT OF MY SOUL'S EXPRESSIONS

You can support your soul's developing expressions by learning to nurture your true nature. This means that you make time to include what you love in your life. When you do so, invigorated energy is caused to overflow into all areas of your life and affect everything you do.

Know what feels true to you - Learn from the intuitive and gut responses you experience as you go about your day. Begin trusting these. Make a point to follow through on your hunches.

Know what type of environment(s) supports you - Notice which environment(s) support your well-being. Allow yourself the space and time to be nurtured by these.

Know what you enjoy - Pay attention to the times you are enjoying yourself. Include more of these experiences within your life.

Know what sparks your passion - What really and truly ignites you? Your passion is a road map leading you to your soul's calling. Try new and different things to find this out. How might you invite your passion into your life, your work, and your relationships?

The whole idea is to provide an atmosphere conducive toward enjoyable, spontaneous, and uninhibited self-expression. The soul loves fun and the freedom to creatively express itself. Make the time to really get to know your Self in relationship to yourself, to others, and to the environment so you can foster the magnificent expressions of your soul. It is time to enliven your spirit!

HEALING

Healing is peace of mind. Healing is balance and harmony. Health is a balanced state of inner peace. We have access to this harmony within our life as we understand the healing abilities of our inner wisdom and truths. As age old wisdom tells us, "The truth shall set you free." When we learn about the truth of our own ability to effect healing, we can bask in the freedom these healing abilities bring to us.

Health is dependent upon our responsibility. We have the responsibility to seek appropriate attention when we are feeling sick. We may seek traditional medical attention, we may work with an alternative or holistic practitioner, or we may employ herbal remedies. Whatever form we choose is dependent upon the ailment, the condition, and our beliefs. Each tradition has its time and place, but ultimately, it is up to the individual to seek the particular care. However, the type of healing that focuses upon removal of symptoms is not the focus of this section. The type of healing that will be discussed is not about someone being "sick" and needing to be "fixed." The healing covered in this section refers to the peace of mind and the well-being that is felt when there is a sense of love enveloping and embracing ourself. This healing refers to a spiritual healing that transcends the physical, yet also affects it.

WHAT IS THE NATURE OF ILLNESS AND DIS-EASE?

Illness results when we are not at ease with ourself and/or our surrounding environment. When we are in a disharmonious relationship or out of balance with our physical, emotional, mental, and spiritual selves, we are more susceptible to "dis-ease." This is because we are not "at ease" with these components of our existence. Therefore, we experience a lack of ease. Not being in harmony with these components is when microorganisms can affect our sense of well-being because any disharmony can cause a breakdown in our system. Faulty beliefs can cause disease. For example, many of us become susceptible to colds and flues regularly because we believe in all of the collective beliefs surrounding these illnesses. We learn to believe in the annual flue season and in the office virus that is going around. Remember, we will attract to us what we believe. Our cultural beliefs and collective programming about pathology affect our well-being. Our beliefs about our faith or lack of faith affect our well-being.

By just thinking positive thoughts, we cannot merely release ourself from the affliction of dis-ease and the nature of illness. Thinking

positive thoughts is merely part of the picture. Thinking positive

thoughts is about attending to the mental aspect of ourself, but since we

are also physical human beings, we must attend to our physical needs as

well. However, we must attend to our emotional, mental, and spiritual

selves in addition to the physical Self. All of these aspects are

important. Now, when we feel in harmony with ourself and within our

environment on all of these levels, then our ability to maintain a literal

sense of well-being is readily available. When we feel this harmony and

balance between all of these levels, we then find ourself more able to

deal with life's stresses, whether the stress presents itself in the form of

a job, a relationship, a belief, or a microorganism. As a result, our body

is less susceptible to stresses causing dis-ease.

When we are struck with dis-ease, pathology, or sickness, it is a

result of our body on at least one of the four levels, trying to release as

well as notify ourself of this intruding imbalance. The sickness in itself

becomes a sounding alarm to bring a conscious awareness of this

imbalance to the stricken individual. To feel this sickness does not mean

that we were bad and are being punished for our trespasses.

Succumbing to illness does not imply that we just did not do a good

enough job of thinking positively. It does not mean that we are to

blame if we cannot prevent or rid ourself of the presenting illness. But

what it does mean is that the sickness presenting itself is our human way of helping ourself attempt to restore a sense of balance within our body. The pathology and the symptoms we are presented with are the manner in which our body attempts to restore balance and harmony. The symptoms are the attempts by the pathology, itself, to struggle to regain balance and to notify ourself that a cleansing is underway. It draws our attention into the space within ourself where our presence is needed.

Sometimes a body that is dis-eased, impaired, and ill never regains that sense of physical balance that might have been present before the symptoms appeared. Instead, the dis-ease remains and asks the individual to discover harmony within oneself in new ways. This means the dis-ease is present and stays for whatever reason. It is as if the dis-ease is a calling and a challenge to find harmony and peace within oneself in ways possibly not explored before. In this case, an absence of dis-ease may not be possible, but a sense of harmony still is.

When we heal we regain a sense of peace within ourself. We can heal on many different levels, but can still be stricken with dis-ease. Healing is equated with peacefulness. Healing is about finding peace within oneself and with oneself. Obtaining a sense of harmony within means finding the peace inside. It may or may not mean absence of illness, impairment, or pathology, but it does mean acquiring a new sense of "ease" with oneself. In the midst of dis-ease a sense of ease can still be found.

Chapter 9 - CONNECTIVE CREATIVITY

When we acknowledge our interconnection with All-That-Is, we begin experiencing a peace of being. Our mere existence seems to hold great importance and incredible potential. We accept this. We no longer fight our spiritual connection within the great web of life. We begin living freely and purposely within our true, inherent power. We not only understand our creative responsibility, but we know ourself as spiritual, creative beings in addition to our humanness. "We are not human beings having a spiritual experience. We are spiritual beings having a human experience," according to Pierre Teilhard de Chardin, a 20th century French Roman Catholic priest and paleontologist. We accept this as we come to know it.

Feeling centered within our own power is the key to empathic understanding. We feel connected when we empathize. With this key of empathy in hand, we now find many doors that can be opened. Strength from our interconnections allows us to walk across each threshold and face whatever prevails. We feel confident to step forward with empathy for our own plight and for those of others. This understanding brings us to view and experience life in its interconnected fashion. We now accept this awareness into our life and become aware of our true abilities as co-creators with the Universal flow.

We learn that the more in tune we feel with ourself, the more in synch we can feel with our surroundings. When we feel in tune, we become increasingly aware of life's synchronicities. We notice the manifestations of the creative visions we keep. We are creative partners with life. No longer do we feel like victims of destiny. We know that we have choice and the freedom to exercise it. Most importantly, we learn to flow with life.

A powerful image to envision while exploring connective creativity is the image of a CROWN. Imagine an exquisite crown sitting upon your head. It encircles your head with a glowing light. The radiant beauty of this crown represents your induction into the realm of greater consciousness. The crown, itself, represents your anointment with the power to become aware of your true Self. Deep in your heart, you have always known your true Self. Now, you allow its expression. You awaken your abilities and you embody your creative genius.

One way to experience the connective encounter of our creativity with All-That-Is is through a visualization exercise. The following exercise helps us increase the awareness of our creative and spiritual connection with the flow of the Universe. This exercise helps us remember our divine and important intent.

Directions -

The Crown Visualization
(For connecting)

As with the other meditative exercises employing relaxation or hypnotic suggestions, allow yourself to get comfortable and free from distractions.

Gently close your eyes. Focus on your breathing and follow your breath in and out, in and out. Take slow and deliberate breaths. Use each breath to help you relax, deeper and deeper, down, down, down. Take your time. (Pause.) As you relax, focus your awareness at the center of your being. You know where this space is within yourself. Trust and go there. This is a safe and nurturing space. You feel warm and centered. Notice a warm and inviting light residing within this space. As you focus on the light, it expands. This light is healing and empowering. You bask in its rays. Imagine the light expanding even more. It fills the space. It fills the center of your being. Watch as it expands into other areas of your body. Take your time. (Pause.) Feel its warmth radiate throughout your physical body. Feel the energy permeate your skin. The light, now, encircles your body. You feel enveloped by the warm light. Now, bring your awareness to the top of your head. This is the place of your crown. Imagine your crown opening up. When it opens, you become a channel of higher consciousness. You are protected and safe within the embrace of your own light. You welcome the pure, universal light to pour into your being. It enters through the crown and washes down your body, inside and out. It merges with your own light. You are connected to the

Universal flow. You radiate with its creative energy. You embody it and channel it. Experience this connection in your own way. Take your time. (Pause.) Know that this connection you are experiencing is everlasting and infinite. The source is omnipotent and omnipresent. Know that you are always connected to it. And know that you can consciously channel it increasingly into your life. All it takes is a purposeful awareness and a willingness to connect. Feel the energy. Enjoy the energy. Be aware of any information or sensations that may arise at this time. Absorb what you experience. (Pause.) When you feel complete with the exercise, allow yourself to bring your focus back to the visual image of a crown sitting upon your head. Let this crown serve as a reminder of your interconnection with All-That-Is. You have free will to welcome the light through your crown and into your awareness. You are always protected by your own light and by the glory of your crown. Bring your awareness back to the center of your being. Know that you can return to this space whenever you like. It is your own sacred and precious center. Bring your attention back to your breathing. Bring your awareness back to your body and to your environment. Take your time. (Pause.) When you are ready, open your eyes and stretch. Welcome back.

BEING IN TUNE
Being "in tune" means being in synch. Synchronizing ourself with the natural rhythms of our body, the environment, the planets, and

others within our life brings harmony to our world. In order to do so, we must first become aware of our patterns. This means becoming aware of our own, personal cycles.

Are you more of a morning person? Or more of a night owl?

Does your body function more efficiently on many small meals consistently eaten throughout the day? Or on three large meals?

Do you tend to be a high strung person bothered by daily problems? Or a mellow person unmoved by aggravating situations?

Are you more creatively productive mid-morning? Or awaken to creative inspiration in the middle of the night?

What other specific patterns are you aware of within your life that seem to affect your daily living?

In answering these questions you will probably find that you fall somewhere in between the examples mentioned. Each one of us has our own place upon these continuums. It is important that we recognize these differences while honoring our own rhythms. When we become aware of our unique and personal flow of rhythms, we can allow our life to be planned according to these cycles. We can establish our life schedule according to our own rhythms instead of attempting to fit ourself into a prescribed, popular melody. We have our own song with its inherent tune, sung at its own key and to its own rhythm, that sounds the best when not reworked. This rhythm, our personal rhythm, must be honored. When we do so, we allow our creative energy to flow more effortlessly and continuously.

There are times (seems like many times!) when we must adhere to an imposed schedule that does not honor our internal timing and specific needs. When this may be the case, however, we can still pay attention to our personal rhythms by taking a few moments, closing our eyes, relaxing with several breaths, and just paying attention to our inner presence. Just notice how you are feeling, what you are thinking, and then let it go. Return to your present environment. The important element here is recognizing our existence that transcends the roles and relationships we play. If we know that eating several small meals throughout the day keeps our energy elevated, then do just that. If we know that much of our creative inspiration comes to us during our sleep, then get in the habit of keeping a dream journal and allowing extra time in the morning for transcribing these nocturnal messages. The key is to honor these rhythms by including them within our life in whatever manner we can.

Our rhythms and cycles will change over the years as our bodies change, as our mental and emotional selves change, and as our spiritual beliefs change. We must give credence to our differences, as well as to our evolving rhythms. By honoring our differences, we are learning to be more attuned to our own internal processes. Thus, we open ourself to a full life of creative expression. This creative energy can come in the form of increased energy, a relaxed disposition, a focused awareness, clear intentions, increased sense of harmony and balance, increased ability to flow with life's circumstances, divine inspiration, intuitive insight, and a developing spiritual understanding.

Once we feel more established and aware of our own cycles and rhythms, we can reach out and increase our conscious awareness of the cycles and rhythms occurring around us. When we are more attuned with ourself, we are more readily able to be attuned with others. This means being able to find harmonious ways to interact with that which is outside of ourself. This includes our relationship with others and with the environment.

Being in tune means that we will be more attuned to reading and interpreting the subtle signals that others send out. This may be in the form of body language, flux and intonation of voice, and gut reactions. We begin to understand the things that are not said, but are, nevertheless, communicated. We begin to sense this not only in others, but within the environment around us. We can increase our ability to be more attuned with the changes in weather, for example, much like the animal kingdom is aware of the changes in seasons. When winter approaches, the animals prepare accordingly. We could prepare for the winter of our life accordingly as well. In preparation, we could learn to speak more openly about approaching our physical mortality. If this was so, death would not seem so frightening because emphasis would be placed upon allowing and accepting its transition. Being more aware of the influence the movement of the planets has upon us can help us understand how we are a part of a bigger system. We can learn to sense the emitted vibrations of the earth, feel her pain, as well as her glory.

The more attuned we become within, the more in synch we become without. They are in a direct proportional ratio to each other. Whether we are in harmony with our own cycles or those outside of us really doesn't matter as they are actually one and the same. When we learn to be attuned to the cycles within our own experience of our human form and spirit, we are learning to be in harmony with the world as a whole. Our experience is a microcosm of the larger world.

The more in-synch we are with our personal cycles, the freer our creative expression becomes because the natural tendency for our creative energy to express itself is in the form of rhythms. These rhythms correlate with rhythms of increased energy whether they be of physical energy, vivid dreams, guiding intuition, or inspiring ideas. The results of increased energy will bring increased creative expression. This means being able to express more fully the true expansiveness of our soul, being able to express who we truly are.

SYNCHRONICITY

The Universe has a rhythm, her own poetic ballad. The manifestation of very meaningful "coincidences," known as synchronicities, display the interconnectedness of this Universal ballad.

Possibly, there is no such thing as a coincidence. We have become accustomed to labeling unexplained and meaningful events as pure coincidence. Most of us grow up learning that we are individuals separated by our flesh, religiosity, culture, ethnicity, and race. We don't learn that events and happenings within our life may have purposeful meanings as well as confirming connections. We don't look for these events in our life. Therefore, when they occur and we experience them, we tend to call them mere coincidences, fortuities, and pure luck.

A synchronistic event is an event that cannot be attributed to chance alone due to its unusual, yet meaningful significance. The synchronistic event helps confirm to us that we are on our path. It signals to us the workings of a higher, Universal intelligence. When a synchronistic event occurs, it is as if this higher intelligence is addressing us personally and specifically. It brings a validating awareness to the state of our present affairs by reminding us of our interconnection within the Universe. The synchronistic event provides us a sneak peak into our interrelations with spirit. This is the domain where we can experience our connections with All-That-Is.

HOW DO I INCREASE SYNCHRONICITY WITHIN MY LIFE?

Synchronistic events occur naturally and spontaneously to the mind that is open to connections and sensitive to patterns. By just being aware that these events do indeed happen, we will increasingly tend to notice when they do so. The more we explore their inherent, specific meaning within our life, the more we find them showing up. We can even create conscious intentions to draw these experiences into our life.

The following are suggestions to use in order to increase the experience of synchronicities within your life.

Be open to possibilities - Believe that help, inspiration, and other resources are anywhere and everywhere.

Tune out distractions - Refrain from destructive and numbing behaviors and actions that keep you from spirit.

Use hindsight - Notice how a chain of events is all connected.

Notice - Explore how things are presently unfolding.

Ask for assistance - Invite synchronicity into your life through your intentions.

TRANS-AWARENESS

Our awareness is a phenomenon that is not just limited, as it seems, to the physical, human body. For the most part, we tend to believe that what we are able to do is limited by our human form and sensory faculties. We tend to believe that our awareness has something to do with our five senses, and is therefore connected to the mechanisms of organs controlled by our brain. Because the brain is a physical organ located in the head, we tend to think that awareness is located in our head, in our brain. Awareness, however, like our mind, is something that is not tangible within our body; in fact, it transcends our

body. Thus, I have coined the term "trans-awareness" to name the
phenomenon I will be discussing. *Trans* meaning *above* and *beyond,*
transcending, and *awareness* meaning *a conscious knowing*.

An experience of trans-awareness is a special type of
synchronistic happening. Synchronicities occur all of the time as they
are of a spontaneous nature. They confirm the interconnection of all
things within the Universe. On the other hand, a trans-awareness event
occurs when a conscious connection is formed with another person. In
other words, a connection between two people's awareness has been
purposely cultivated and established through their relationship with one
another. When the meaning of the synchronistic event has deepened
and has become increasingly personal, precise, and specific, we are now
in the midst of a trans-awareness occurrence.

At times we may have the feeling that someone is looking at us.
When we have this feeling, we tend to turn in the direction from which it
is coming and find that someone is, indeed, looking at us. This is an
example of awareness, a trans-awareness. We don't have physical eyes
in the back of our head that can see this person who is looking at us.
Instead, we just sense it and feel it. This awareness is a sensing and a
feeling that transcends the five senses and goes beyond the experience
of the human form.

We are all connected within a matrix of energy/light that is
vibrating at various speeds. The fact that I can sense somebody looking

at me when my back is turned to them is an example of this connection. These implications show us that if we just think a thought about someone or something, we influence a reaction from and within the object of our thought. When we intend to do something, whether it be looking, smelling, touching, tasting, hearing, we are, in a sense, interacting and receiving an exchange of energy from the object we are focused on experiencing. This exchange of energy is our connection. This exchange of energy is the connecting force between all of us. This energy is generally not detected by our five senses, but by our sixth sense, the intuitive sense (discussed in Chapter 8).

Exploring this concept further, our awareness has the ability to be in many locations at the same time. Multi-awareness means having the ability to be aware in many different places simultaneously. This phenomenon is commonly understood by many indigenous people world-wide. An aspect of our consciousness can be with others regardless of the space and time continuum. This aspect can also become a part of the other person's awareness. For example, you may be thinking about someone and shortly after, you receive a letter or a phone call from this individual. You may be wanting to take up a new hobby or sport and soon you are presented the opportunity to do so. It may come in the form of a community class mailing or it may come in the form of meeting someone who already enjoys that activity and is willing to help you. The possibilities are endless! It seems as if someone has read your mind and basically, that's what has happened. You sent out the intention and you received a response. When the intention is set forth, a response gravitates toward the intention, toward the intended thought and/or action. Here is another example of what this concept trans-awareness entails. Let's say you are engaged in an activity that may be new and foreign to yourself and you think about another individual you know who is already adept at this particular activity. Immediately, you begin to sense this individual's presence or hear his/her voice in your head. This presence offers words of encouragement and suggestions for succeeding at this particular activity. All of this can occur if we can banish our own self-doubts and limited thinking.

Not too long ago, I had a personal experience with a trans-awareness event. A friend of mine who lives about 2,000 miles away from me was in a bookstore. She came across a section of books that she knows I find interesting. She felt this overwhelming desire within herself, pulling her to purchase a specific book for me. The book was an expensive book, but nonetheless, the urge to buy the book for me was so powerful that she went ahead and made the purchase. Soon after, she told me that she had something to give me that she felt inclined to buy. However, she did not send it to me until about one and a half months later due to what she interpreted as her procrastination. It turns out that when I did receive the book from her, it pertained exactly to information I was currently needing. It fit right in with my work and helped me explore my current undertakings further. I believe that if she would have sent me the book a month and a half earlier when she had originally purchased it, I would not have been ready for all of the information. The fact that she withheld sending me that book gave me the opportunity to prepare myself for its reading.

There are no "chance" happenings. I believe that since she and I have a great connection through our supportive friendship to each other, that a part of my awareness was with her. My awareness was that overwhelming urge that she experienced, encouraging her to stop, see this book, and purchase it for me. Talk about being able to ask for what you want! This part of our awareness has no inhibitions. My consciousness was with her and became part of her awareness, but only because we have a connection and we are both open to feeling, hearing, and honoring this connection.

I don't think my friend would have had the trans-awareness experience if we did not already have a conscious connection, and thus, a conscious influence on each other. The fact that she thought of me while she was browsing certain books is related to the conscious influence we share. I have shared before with her what type of books I like. So, no surprise that she might think of me at that moment. The fact that she felt an overwhelming urge to purchase a specific and relevant book for me takes this awareness deeper. This illustration speaks for the phenomenon of trans-awareness. She had an awareness, transcending a conscious knowing, to buy and send the book to me when she did. However, the book itself, her conscious struggle, and the delayed receipt of the book was just perfect! I attribute these workings to both, a conscious influence and a beyond-conscious influence, thus, a trans-awareness.

We can go through life without developing and furthering these connections with others, but they exist, nonetheless. We may only consciously experience these types of occurrences every now and then. When we are aware of these happenings, we increase our abilities to work with this connective matrix at will. This is not to say that this concept of trans-awareness interferes with others against their own free will, but this awareness and connection will be received when the recipient and the sender are both open, aware, and welcoming of this type of connection. Being conscious of our trans-awareness, helps us to understand more fully our connection to All-That-Is. This awareness helps explain how our thoughts, actions, and intentions influence and create reactions in the object of our focus. This teaches us that we are all connected in exalted ways.

PEACE OF MIND AND SPIRIT
As we learn to feel centered within ourself, we find ourself resonating more and more with our own truths. We wholeheartedly and happily learn to be ourself as we accept our journey in life. Not only is it possible to accept our path, but we learn to appreciate the unique and

specific characteristics and qualities that make us who we are. We see the truth within ourself and we accept it, whether or not we like it. This means we learn to see past our so-called "imperfections" and accept these as a part of our individual perfection. When this is the case, our expression becomes a truthful one making the unfolding of our creative expansion more and more possible.

Life's ups and downs don't go away. There will always be hurdles to jump, obstacles to face, mountains to climb, and challenges to meet. Integration of these concepts and an honest acceptance of yourself will make the difference. Instead of endlessly and hopelessly fleeing from, struggling over, fighting with, and worrying about these situations, you will begin to find yourself approaching many of these happenings in a new light. Soon, you realize that life will contain tension and friction. You understand that you will experience myriad emotions. However, you know that nothing and no one can make you be other than you are. With this knowledge you accept self-responsibility to live the life your soul needs. You develop a strong sense of who you are intact with the interconnections you have with All-That-Is. You create your world from within and experience it from without. You feel empowered, yet humble, as you continually strive to know and experience your truths. Life is just one level of experience and you flow.

WHAT DOES IT MEAN TO FLOW?
Flow is seemingly effortless movement. It is all around us in

nature. Trees bend and sway, flowing with the breeze. Ocean tides flow according to the gravitational pull of the moon and sun. Animals in the wild live their lives following the flow of the changing seasons. Flow is a very natural process. When we are in the flow, we are focused on the process of our journey, not the outcome or destination. We bend, we sway; you might say we become quite flexible. We follow our natural tide and we honor the seasonal changes in our body and in our life.

The experience of flow means being in synch with the heartbeat of life, not fighting against the current, not trying to dam it up or make it flow in an unnatural direction, but flowing <u>with</u> it. That means giving into ourself and allowing the full, creative spirit to be exposed and expressed. This means allowing whatever is inside to be explored. It means flowing with the processes that occur in our life. It means feeling, believing, and knowing that all is in place, that all is just the way it should be, and that there is a rhyme and reason to "this madness" we sometimes feel we are experiencing.

All things flow from the energy of creation. We can learn to allow the energy of manifestation and creativity to flow through us. Our journey flows as we begin to understand the principles of creation and how these concepts are affecting our life and the lives of others. Many of us have studied the various principles for creating the reality we want. Creating what you want is similar to creating with the flow, but there are also major differences. When we attempt to create what we want, we assume we know what is best for ourself and the situation we are trying

to manifest. By doing so, we are attempting to control the situation. In

the book <u>Creative</u> <u>Visualization</u>, Shakti Gawain reminds us that "The

[U]niverse may be trying to show you something better that you haven't

even considered." Now, there is nothing wrong with wanting and

desiring a better life or a better way for ourself and for others.

However, we cut ourself off from the flow when we dictate what we

desperately want and think we must have, because then we may not get

what we truly need for our highest good. For instance, if we ask for just

enough money to pay our monthly bills, then we tend to find ourself

doing just that. The Universe laughs as she knows this irony all too well.

What she really wanted to provide you with was the winning lottery

ticket, but you canceled the flow of receiving it when you just knew what

you wanted. Of course, this is an extreme example, but it's important to

understand that there is a way to create with the flow without limiting

ourself. We can shift from asking "for what" we want to asking "for what

is best for my highest good." Since we don't readily know the bigger

picture of our life's unfolding, we might as well learn to trust this great

mystery. This means creating our reality through our beliefs, choices,

and actions, but living in grace with the flow. In this regard, the

experience of flow includes both a conscious attempt to master

situations and a process of surrendering and letting go. It is a fine line

and a delicate dance we must do, but only you will know where to step.

We learn to flow with our journey as we begin to understand more about ourself and others. Flowing means to be with the current, be with the choices, and be in the present. However, "going with the flow" is not the same as "being in the flow." Going with the flow denotes a passive stance. In fact, the experience of flow involves a very active stance for the Self. Flow is not a free ride!

It means not jumping ahead and worrying about what could, should, or might happen. It doesn't mean dreading what happened in the past, who did what to whom, who did what to you, but it does mean being in the present and being with the flow of things. Flow means just that, flow! Things can flow in and out of our life. For example, you begin to notice the synchronistic meetings you are having with people. You know that you want to meet somebody and then the opportunity presents itself. You think about somebody and then that person calls. You more readily encounter the concept of trans-awareness as you learn to experience life beyond your typical levels of conscious awareness. The examples are limitless, but these are just a few ways the flow manifests within our life. If we are with the flow, we can utilize the flow, we can be a part of the flow, we can be one with the flow to allow ourself to move closer and closer to our creative essence. The more we give into the flow, the more it actually allows us to open to our strengths and to the divine, creative spark within ourself.

Like Zen Philosophy, being in the flow means we do not have to do anything or try to be anything; it means that we just are and there's an acceptance of this. Wherever we are on our path, is just where we need to be. It does not mean that there is a resignation to the miserable experiences we have felt and to the current unbearable and uncomfortable situations we find ourself within. What does develop is an acceptance of who we are, where we've been, and where we are going. Our choices and the changes they bring are in the present. Flow encourages us to take our active stance through the freedom of choice. Being in the flow is not about negating ourself or harboring past pains and happenstances that we would rather get rid of or would rather disown. It's about letting ourself be and letting others be. It's about being in connection with ourself, and therefore, understanding our connection to others. We are not fighting that inner connection, so we are not fighting that outer connection. As it is within, that's how it is without. How one flows with oneself is in direct relation and proportion to how one flows outwardly with others. So, we can view ourself as a microcosm of our world, a direct reflection of our world and view our interactions with others as a macrocosm, a direct reflection of our inner state of being. As it is in the microcosm is how it is in the macrocosm.

Flowing is about being in harmony with the energy of the Universe. Flowing is about allowing. Flowing is a natural process in which things strive to evolve, grow, and change. We flow more readily and easily when we take down the barriers of judgment and discrimination and choose to view things in ourself with an open mind, a loving heart, and an outstretched hand. The flow continues to expand as we do the same with others.

The key to flowing is summed up by the words "center "and "connection." We become more creative individuals as we learn to center and connect with our natural energy. In actuality, we are just "re-membering" our creative inheritance. We are assembling and integrating the pieces of ourself that have been neglected. This is because we are not forcing anything. We are allowing this creative inheritance to expand, express, and open on its own accord regardless of our time table. Creativity, that life energy inside of us, flows much like a current in a mountain stream. It flows in one direction and that is downstream. It takes the path of least resistance. It becomes stronger and stronger and bigger and bigger as it meets other streams with which it joins forces and flows into rivers, lakes, and various channels, taking the flow further down to the seas. The notion behind this analogy is that the creative energy flows best when it is allowed to take the path of least resistance, when it is allowed to choose its own course, and allowed to exist without imposed obstructions or limitations hampering its way. When we flow like the current, we too allow our creativity to be naturally unleashed because we have released and let go of the obstructions and limitations. We learn to flow with our creative essence, our own piece of the creative Universe, and awaken to the realm of atonement.

WHAT IS AT-<u>ONE</u>-MENT?

In Christianity, Jesus' suffering and death gifted man with his reconciliation with God. This is atonement in the Christian faith. However, this is not a discussion of religion, but a discourse in spirituality. Atonement will be explained on a different level.

Atonement is that space we exist within when we find ourself in agreement with the Universal flow. All flows as one energy. All is of the same energy. We are a part of the unified force and we are the unified force. We don't fully grasp or understand the power that is within and moves through us until we allow this energy to be awakened. It awakens when we find ourself within the flow.

When we move into the awareness of atonement, agreement, we realize that we are in a space where we can comprehend the At-One-Ment of all energy. We begin to understand our connection to All-That-Is. We realize that our creative impulses are connected to the creative impulses of others. We are spiritually connected through giant matrices of energy. Each one of us is a spark of the many within this creative, electrifying field. We are unified with others. Since we are all connected, we come to realize the responsibility we must assume for our thoughts. With this realization, we can learn to work with or against this unifying field, this flow. We understand that life is like a giant tapestry with each one of us woven into the fabric, much like a single thread is woven into its place, creating the overall design of this huge tapestry. The design requires each of the threads to be present and in their place to comprise the overall affect of this giant tapestry. Each thread is unique and follows its own specific pathway through the overall design. We begin to realize that what we are thinking influences the person we are doing the thinking about. We understand the power of prayer and meditation. We learn that our thoughts affect the other people even more than ourself. We have sent the thoughts out with direction and intention. However, the ironic truth informs us that the effects we have had upon another person, in turn, truly affects ourself as well. Humankind has always known the adage, "You shall reap what you sow." We also understand that "like attracts like." We come to understand this principle of cause and effect fully when we become aware of life's interconnections. Threads removed from a tapestry have an effect upon the overall design and value of the tapestry. We recognize this value and begin to have regard for each other. We begin to have reverence for our actions and we begin to take responsibility for them. We understand that creatively we have a responsibility to each other and to ourself. We learn that we can creatively influence situations just by the mere presence of our thoughts and we experience the results. We do have an affect upon this great tapestry of life.

In this awareness, for example, we may begin sharing joint dreams with another. We share dreams because it is within the dream state that our soul exists in limitless form. When we maintain limitless thinking, we experience the extraordinary because we are tapped into the realm of infinite possibilities. We may begin second guessing what another is wanting or needing and present it before this person has even asked or requested such attention. We may awaken to hidden abilities, such as telekinesis and telepathy. We open to many abilities that we once believed to be only of the realm of psychics, sages, and seers. The channel for our creativity expands in many new ways. We uncover these possibilities as we begin to understand that we are all really of one energy, flowing through each of us and interconnecting us through our thoughts and intentions. Therefore, we can effect what appears to be outside of us in the same manner we can control the muscles in our body. At this level we experience creativity as a responsibility and ability to help ourself, which in turn helps others. We recognize the creative spark of all creation as being the same energy and coming from the same place. Understanding this principle of atonement means that we, for instance, have the ability to channel information that has existed before, exists now, and exists in the future. This means we have the ability to tap into the sensations that appear to be outside of us. Through the discipline of the processes of mental focus, physical relaxation, and remaining open, people have been able to communicate with and understand the needs of animals, sense disturbances upon the Earth, and experience sensations emitted by plants.

We learn that our expressed creativity helps others open to their own creativity. We know the existence of this great energy flowing in us, through us, and around us. We learn our own truths and allow these to expand as we follow our soul's calling. We do a great disservice to the Universe if we hide from this divine plan. As we follow our calling, we begin to see that this alliance with and dedication to our soul's purpose helps others open to claiming their own purpose. It becomes contagious.

This is the Law of Critical Mass. A great example of how this works is seen in the hundredth monkey theory. Ken Keyes, author of the book, The Hundredth Monkey, details the true story of how monkeys off the coast of Japan began washing their sweet potatoes in the salt water after mimicking one of the monkeys in their group. Interestingly enough, this same behavior appeared in a group of monkeys who were hundreds of miles away and had no contact with this first group. This illustrates the theory of critical mass, which states that when a certain level of saturation is reached within the consciousness of a species by an optimal amount of individuals, the consciousness of the rest of the species is thereby automatically influenced. This means that we have the ability to influence the state of consciousness of all when enough of us practice the same actions, thoughts and feelings. This demonstrates the fact that our connections run deeply and have great, meaningful potential.

The awareness of how we are all connected as one energy helps us move along our journey rapidly and easily, but not without cost. We must pay by giving up or letting go of the limiting views and beliefs that are prevalent in our life. The views of racism, prejudice, bigotry, and separatism must be released. The beliefs of incompetence, helplessness, and judgment must be shed. Our purpose here on earth is to re-experience our interconnection and re-expand the channels of our abilities to share of ourself. We know this stuff. These creative channels that we try so hard to find and search every where for, are within. They are of the realm of love, for the love of Self and for the love of others.

May we always find the courage to seek our truths and the freedom to express them. I invite you to create and bring forth forevermore!

And Spirit patiently waits...

GLOSSARY

<u>All-That-Is</u> - every single thing is a part of the divine essence comprising the eternal Universe. It is all of creation.

<u>At-one-ment</u> - flowing in agreement with the unified force of the Universe.

<u>Chaos</u> - the formless darkness from which all of creation is birthed.

<u>Dark night of the soul</u> - sheer hopelessness and despair, where the ego renounces the illusion of control.

<u>Dis-ease</u> - a lack of ease with any number of components within our life.

<u>Ego</u> - a construct of our human form that operates in consciousness and unconsciousness. It provides us with a sense of stability and structure for how we view ourself and our world.

<u>Higher Self</u> - the voice of our soul.

<u>Inner Self</u> - the voice of our inner knowing.

<u>Mind's eye</u> - the internal construct which allows us to receive and process mental images.

<u>Re-member</u> - the process of piecing back together who we are and what we already know.

<u>Self</u> - the archetypal blueprint of ourself that exists in perfection and potentiality, our wholeness.

<u>Soul</u> - the individualized hologram of the divine essence.

<u>Spirit</u> - the breath of life, the energy of the Universe.

<u>Third eye</u> - the center for higher consciousness, located midway between the eyebrows and above the bridge of the nose.

<u>Uni-verse</u> - an energetically alive and harmonious arrangement in which life exists.

<u>Visualization</u> - the projection experienced by the mind's eye.

SELECTED BIBLIOGRAPHY

Fox, Matthew. <u>Original Blessing</u>. Santa Fe, NM.: Bear & Company, Inc., 1983.

Gawain, Shakti. <u>Creative Visualization</u>. Mill Valley, Calif.: Whatever Publishing, 1978.

Casarjian, Robin. <u>Forgiveness</u>. New York: Bantam Books, 1992.

Small, Jacquelyn. <u>Embodying Spirit</u>. New York: HarperCollins Publishers, Inc., 1994.

Griscom, Chris. <u>The Healing of Emotion</u>. New York: Simon & Schuster, 1988.

Capra, Fritjof. <u>The Tao of Physics</u>. 3rd ed. Boston: Shambala Publications, Inc., 1991.

Dyer, Wayne. <u>You'll See it When You Believe it</u>. New York: William Morrow and Company, Inc., 1989.

---. <u>Your Sacred Self: Making the Decision to be Free</u>. New York: HarperCollins Publishers, Inc., 1995.

---. <u>Real Magic: Creating Miracles in Everyday Life</u>. New York: HarperCollins Publishers, Inc., 1992.

Zukov, Gary. <u>Seat of the Soul</u>. New York: Simon & Schuster, 1989.

Keyes, Ken. <u>The Hundreth Monkey</u>. 3rd ed. St. Mary, Ky.: Vision Books, 1981.

Johnson, Robert. <u>Owning Your Own Shadow</u>. New York: HarperCollins Publishers, Inc., 1991.

Csikszentmihalyi, Mihaly. <u>Flow: The Psychology of Optimal Experience</u>. New York: HarperCollins Publishers, Inc., 1990.

Jung, Carl G. <u>Memories, Dreams, Reflections</u>. Rev. ed. Recorded and edited by Aniela Jaffe, New York: Vintage Books, 1965.

Sherwood, Keith. <u>The Art of Spiritual Healing</u>. St. Paul, Minn.: Llewellyn Publications, 1989.

Chopra, Deepak. <u>Quantum Healing: Exploring the Frontiers of Mind/Body</u>. New York: Bantam Books, 1989.

ABOUT THE AUTHOR

Karen A. Dahlman believes that self-empowerment is the key to living a richly rewarding and authentic life. All of her education, life & career experiences and the companies she developed and owned, center around the theme of living a bountiful life through creatively pushing boundaries and expressing inner potentials. She lives a life, co-existing between right-brain and left-brain functioning, all the while aligning within a dynamic heart/brain interplay with her heart being the leader.

Ms. Dahlman received her B.A. and M.A. degrees from the University of New Mexico. She began her professional career as an art psychotherapist, licensed counselor, hypnotherapist, and artist back in 1987. For over a decade, she worked within multiple settings, with varying populations, including her private practice and public workshops, while providing creative and expressive means for her clients to find health. She emerged as an accomplished leader within the art therapy world.

After undergoing a life-changing event that left her penniless, she relocated to Southern California and entered the high-technology, telecommunication industry without any prior knowledge of the skill-sets required. Yet, Ms. Dahlman became founder and CEO of CVC, Inc., a consulting and utility design firm for the fortune 100 wireless carriers, which grossed profits of over one million within two years of opening its doors by employing the principals she writes about in *The Spirit of Creativity; Embodying Your Soul's Passion.* In fact, she wrote her manuscript originally in 1997 to find herself living it out page by page for the following seven years.

Her seven-year journey brought her in touch with internal forces needing to be ingested and incubated within her life before their creative expressions could be witnessed outwardly. Ms. Dahlman writes about these steps in a most prophetic manner that effectively influenced and changed her life forever. There is no way she will ever turn back the pages of her life to a pre-understanding of the principals she writes about in *The Spirit of Creativity.*

Today, Ms. Dahlman resides in the lovely coastal town of San Clemente, CA and remains at the helm of her beloved company, CVC, Inc. She continues to creatively diversify its interests into new industries and challenge herself to express further potentials.

Author contact: PO Box 1496, San Clemente, CA 92674
karen@cvc-group.com

CPSIA information can be obtained at www.ICGtesting.com
Printed in the USA
LVOW10s1944071013

355809LV00018B/1232/P